T0322184

Four Points of the Compass

JERRY BROTTON

Four Points of the Compass

The Unexpected History of Direction

ALLEN LANE
an imprint of
PENGUIN BOOKS

ALLEN LANE

UK | USA | Canada | Ireland | Australia
India | New Zealand | South Africa

Allen Lane is part of the Penguin Random House group of companies
whose addresses can be found at global.penguinrandomhouse.com

First published 2024
002

Copyright © Jerry Brotton, 2024

The moral right of the author has been asserted

Set in Berling Nova Text Pro 10.12/15 pt
by Francisca Monteiro
Printed and bound in Great Britain by Clays Ltd, Elcograf S.p.A.

The authorized representative in the EEA is Penguin Random House Ireland,
Morrison Chambers, 32 Nassau Street, Dublin D02 YH68

A CIP catalogue record for this book is available from the British Library

ISBN: 978-0-241-55687-0

www.greenpenguin.co.uk

MIX
Paper | Supporting
responsible forestry
FSC
www.fsc.org   FSC® C018179

Penguin Random House is committed to a
sustainable future for our business, our readers
and our planet. This book is made from Forest
Stewardship Council® certified paper.

We live . . . lives based upon selected fictions. Our view of reality is conditioned by our position in space and time – not by our personalities as we like to think. Thus every interpretation of reality is based upon a unique position. Two paces east or west and the whole picture is changed.

—Lawrence Durrell, *The Alexandria Quartet* (1957–70)

Nel mezzo del cammin di nostra vita
mi ritrovai per una selva oscura,
ché la diritta via era smarrita

—Dante, *Purgatorio*, Canto I, lines 1–3

For Pen Woods:
the best direction

Contents

List of Illustrations

Photographic ancknowledgements are given in parentheses.

Plates

Illustrations

Acknowledgements

This is one of the shortest books I have written: it was also the hardest, accumulating acknowledgements in inverse proportion to its length. Most of those listed in what follows know that the book was written under the most difficult of personal circumstances. Many of them saw me at my lowest, and for their unstinting kindness, generosity, patience, love and unwavering support in keeping me afloat, I want to thank them all.

The book started life as a BBC Radio 4 series called 'One Direction' inspired by conversations with its producer, Simon Hollis. I am grateful to Simon for making a brilliant series – along with many others we have made – and his friendship and concern during some very tough times. The cartographic history fraternity offered a wealth of advice and references, for which I thank Catherine Delano Smith, Alfred Hiatt, Amani Lusekelo, Alan Millard, Yossie Rapoport and Dan Terkla. Other colleagues also provided invaluable references and insights: thank you Michael Bravo for the North Pole, Caroline Dodds Pennock for Aztec directions, *Felipe Fernández-Armesto for cardinal points*, Robert Macfarlane for thoughtful and generous exchanges especially on the north, Ed Parsons for blue dots, Karen Stern for Hebraic directions, Mojisola Adebayo for the queer poles and Andrea Wulf for Humboldt. My agent George Capel and her team at Georgina Capel Associates were a delight to work with: George managed to be funny, tough and supportive just when required. Students and colleagues on the Mile End Road made work a pleasure under the toughest of circumstances, for which I thank Faisal Abul, Tamara Atkin, Jonathan Boffey, Rupert Dannreuther, Markman

Ellis, Lara Fothergill, Rachael Gilmour, Pat Hamilton, Suzanne Hobson and Bev Stewart.

This is the third book I have written with my editor Stuart Proffitt and throughout he has remained 'as constant as the north star'. As well as being a consummate professional he has been a source of great support in times of personal crisis, for which I am extremely grateful to him. It has been a pleasure to work with Fahad Al-Amoudi, Isabel Blake, Richard Duguid and Vartika Rastogi. Richard Mason did a superb job copyediting the text, and Amanda Russell was a terrific picture researcher. In the US Grove Atlantic have proved to be a fantastic new home for this book and others to come: from the outset working with George Gibson and his team has been an absolute delight. A remarkable array of friends and family have also sustained me throughout. Thanks to my brother Peter and sister Susan for more support than I could have imagined, and the return just in time of my cousin Nicky Berry. I cannot wait to show the book to my daughter Honey, and one day, I hope, to her sister Ruby and brother Hardie. So many dear friends helped more than they know: Bok Goodall, Hayat Kamille, Matthew Dimmock, George Morley, Celine Hispiche, Anthony Sattin, Vik Sivalingam and my teacher Maggie Sheen. Alongside them thanks to Gerald McLean and Donna Landry, fellow Turkish travellers; Paul Heritage for all his love, hope and optimism of the will; Claire Preston, who was always at the end of the line; Hugh McLean who blew back in from the east; Peter Barber, who has supported me with unstinting kindness since I first entered the world of maps thirty years ago, and who read the entire manuscript and offered vital insights; David Schalkwyk, who also read the book and gave me the gift of language games; Natasha Podro, Richard Ovenden, Nick Millea and Rana Mitter for reminding me that Oxford can be a place of ideas; Guy Richards Smit, who has seen all four points of the compass with me and is *still* the wind beneath my wings; Rob Nixon, one of the greatest of friends and closest of readers, who when I lost the line gave me the last dot; Peter Florence, who also read the book in one of my darkest moments, and along with all his love and solace showed me the way; Tim Brook and his wife Fay, dear friends and travellers. Tim has been reading me for many years, and his astute feedback and weekly Zoom calls kept me going when I did not think I could. Rajesh Venugopal is a wonderful friend and has always been there practically and emotionally when I needed it most, as has Krzysztof Dzieciolowski, too far away, but always near at hand. With them came new friends, especially Kate Day and Ili Elia, David Kohn and Margherita Laera, Tonderai Munyevu and Adam McGuigan, Gabs and Jamie Parker, Philip Reeder and Louisa Reeder-Pearson, Alan and Adrienne Russell, Ferdinand Saumarez Smith, Katherine Schofield and Helen Sunderland.

I have been writing acknowledgements to my friend and colleague David Colclough for as long as I can remember, and hopefully this won't be the last: he is the most thoughtful, gentle and loving of friends, who was always there for me whenever I needed it. Daniel Crouch and his wonderful family gave me tough love, great company and a place to stay in extremis. It is difficult to encompass the enduring friendship of Adam Lowe and his wife Charlotte Skene Catling. So much of Adam and his extraordinary work at Factum Arte can be found in this book. As well as being a creative inspiration he has yet again saved me when I fell. I trust I can eventually repay him. Joad Raymond is the best of friends, a second brother who has been there every day for me throughout these last turbulent years, for which I am immensely grateful. How to fully acknowledge the phenomenon Candace Allen? Over the last two years Candace taught me that there is always something to live for: she is a remarkable person and I treasure our beautiful friendship.

It is a huge pleasure to acknowledge the incredible kindness,

ACKNOWLEDGEMENTS

support and love of the Woods family: Jan and Roger Woods, Kathryn Woods and Sebastian Townsend, Steve Woods, Michelle Schramm, and Finn Woods. Jan welcomed me into the family by showing me unconditional love from the moment we met: she is a truly remarkable person. Roger generously let me take the helm of Anam Cara and put the wind back in my sails: I look forward to further travels and discoveries with him. I am very lucky to have both of them in my life.

The book is dedicated to Pen Woods. Pen entered my life when I had lost direction: I have only found it again because of her love, care, kindness, and unwavering commitment to a life of joy and creativity. Pen showed me the Domus Aurea when I had lost sight of such things. She is all my days of miracle and wonder.

Orientation

The Blue Marble

Only twenty-four human beings have ever travelled far enough into outer space to see the Earth as a globe. At 200,000 kilometres from the planet, or over halfway to the Moon, passing between our planet and the Sun, it is possible to see the Earth fully illuminated. When following a polar orbit these astronauts can look down on the Earth from above the North Pole and see the Earth – as with most of the planets in our solar system – rotating on its axis counterclockwise, in what is called a prograde motion, or west to east, the same rotation as that of the Sun. Prograde motion is caused by the momentum of the cloud of gas and dust particles from which the Sun and stars were first formed. As the solar system formed, these rotating particles came together to form a mass that separated into planets, which in turn continued to spin in the same prograde counterclockwise direction (nobody knows why Uranus and Venus are the exceptions, following a retrograde rotation). Watching the Earth rotate, the astronaut could then imagine a line running down through its core, starting at the North Pole and ending at the South Pole. North, south, east and west: nothing seems more natural and universal than these four cardinal directions, either imagining the Earth in your mind, or looking down on it from space.

Yet on 7 December 1972, one astronaut took a photograph of the Earth with a very different orientation (Plate 1). NASA's Apollo 17, with its three-man crew of Eugene A. Cernan, Ronald

E. Evans and Harrison H. Schmitt, was the most recent space mission to put humans on the Moon. Just over five hours into the mission, around 29,000 kilometres from the Earth, one of the astronauts looked out of the window and saw the planet fully illuminated by the Sun's light. He reached for a Hasselblad camera, which was part of the mission's scientific equipment, and snapped four photographs of the Earth, each less than a minute apart, adjusting the exposure after the first shot to provide the second, sharper, defining image. What they captured was a breathtaking vision of Earth, shining white clouds curling over and across the cobalt-blue oceans, the verdant green belt of tropical rainforests in central Africa and Madagascar contrasting with the arid Arabian peninsula, and the snow-white Antarctic appearing to gently cradle our beautiful, fragile world.

All three astronauts subsequently claimed they took the photograph, and for good reason: it soon became one of history's most famous and reproduced images. NASA designated the photo AS17-148-22727 and attributed it to the entire crew. The photograph soon became known as 'the blue marble' shot, the first of the whole Earth and the only one so far taken. When NASA released the photo, its worldwide impact was immediate and profound. It inspired an environmental movement driven by a sense of humanity's singular, collective fragility, inhabiting the exquisite blue planet, Earth, seen from space for the first time and framed by the black and inhospitable void of outer space. The image generated calls for global togetherness and ecological humility by reorienting how we thought about our species and our planetary obligations.

But when NASA first developed the photograph, they saw what they regarded as a problem: it had been taken with the South Pole at the top of the frame swathed in cloud, Africa in the middle and the Arabian Peninsula at the bottom. The camera was being held by a weightless astronaut who could not distinguish up from down at the moment he pressed the shutter. Concerned that the photo might disorient viewers' expectations of what the world looked like, NASA inverted the image, to align it with most people's assumptions that the North Pole should be at the top and the South Pole at the bottom. The world was literally turned upside down: but which way up is true? The story of the world's most reproduced image of itself shows that there is no universal frame of reference from which to determine absolute direction – even in outer space. All four directions can only be understood from your point of observation, which is defined by where you stand on or above the globe. Reverse the north and south axes – as effectively happened with the Apollo 17 photograph – invert 'up' and 'down', and the Earth would appear to rotate clockwise from east to west.[1]

As NASA's treatment of the Blue Marble photograph shows, most contemporary societies tend to orient their mental and graphic geography with north at the top. But this has not always been the case, and some societies established south or east as their cardinal directions; their languages and beliefs still reflect such orientation. These four apparently simple and universally accepted terms are far more subjective and specific to time, place, language and culture than we might realize. There is no reason why north should necessarily sit at the top of modern world maps (or photographs): south would do just as well. But the story of *why* north triumphed lies at the heart of this book.

*

The cardinal directions are relative terms, but over centuries they have become established markers of not just *where* we are in the world, but *who* we are. Early cultures located themselves within their immediate environment: wherever they lived on the planet, people could observe the Sun rising in the direction many named east (or its variants) and watch it setting in the direction they called west. East to west was probably the earliest prime axis that people understood by simply watching the Sun's path across the sky. The worship of the Sun, or heliolatry, characterized ancient Egyptian worship of several solar deities: *Horus* (the rising Sun), *Ra* (the noon Sun) and *Osiris* (the dying or setting Sun). On the other side of the world Incan religious cults were also dedicated to Sun worship. Temples in Peru's Machu Picchu citadel contained stone guide posts called *Inti-huatana* (translated as the 'hitching post of the Sun'), which marked the winter solstice festival of *Inti Raymi*. But this horizontal solar axis was eventually followed by understanding another vertical axis running north to south, which could be identified by observing both the Sun and the stars. At noon the Sun is always due south in the northern hemisphere and due north in the southern hemisphere. The north–south axis also finds its horizontal confirmation in the night sky. Living in the northern hemisphere, you can look up at the stars and find north according to *Polaris*, the North or Pole Star. Perpendicular to the north is south. If you live in the southern hemisphere, that direction is identified by *Polaris Australis*, the South Star. Combining the two axes – east–west horizontally and north–south vertically – creates four cardinal directions.

The word 'cardinal' comes from the Latin *cardinalis*, meaning 'hinge', and something of fundamental importance. The cardinal directions are therefore central or pivotal points or principles on which orientation depends; yet, like any hinge, they can move backwards and forwards as relative positions and come to mean their opposite. This is the enduring paradox of the four cardinal directions: they appear to be real and natural, yet they are invented and cultural; they exist in nearly every society, yet can mean exactly their opposite, depending on where you are and what language you speak.

The cardinal directions actually pre-date the invention of the four points of the compass, in which a magnetized needle aligns itself with the Earth's geomagnetic field. Instead they were based initially on a combination of ancient astronomical observations, physical distinctions and meteorological experience, including the winds. This apparently simple yet absolute system of classification provides humans with a basic method of physical coordination in the space around them: without directions, we would be lost.

There is a physical reality to the four directions: we see the Sun rise and set and label them east and west; we can observe the position of the midday Sun or *Polaris*, or look at a compass and designate the directions as north and (by implication) south. But each direction is meaningless without language. Someone points in one direction and says, 'That is east', or any one of the other three cardinal directions. As we shall see, once language becomes part of naming the four directions, rules of their usage and meaning are established that shift and change over time and in different societies as each direction takes on alternative meanings – sometimes even exact opposites – depending on how groups of people change and adapt attitudes about the natural world and the words they use to describe it.

Just as language is subject to evolution and interpretation, so too, it transpires, are the four directions. North changes over time depending on whether you calculate it using the stars, a map or a magnetic compass (but more of that later). The word 'north' never corresponds uniformly over time to one thing or place. Instead it can mean different things depending on where you are. In the UK the north carries associations of deprivation and economic underdevelopment; in Italy and the USA quite the opposite is true: the north is a place of prosperity and urban sophistication. All the cardinal directions are subject to change and adaptation based on how they are used in what some

5

philosophers and linguists call 'language games': the rules and conventions upon which languages rely for them to be understood and acted on by their speakers.[2]

The meaning of words like 'east' or 'west' are only understood by their use in the rules and 'games' established in any language at a given point and in a specific place. Language requires rules to underlie all the possible applications of a word or cluster of words – like the four cardinal directions. Grasping these rules – like the rules of any game – means knowing how to use such words in different contexts: one may be an astronomical context, and another a religious, economic, philosophical or, of course, geographical one. But when 'south' means different and often contradictory things to different people, it is not a matter of arbitrary personal opinion: instead, the word's meaning operates according to the rules of the particular language game it inhabits, which are also subject to change and adaptation, but which can only be altered in relation to and with other communities. This book does not reveal any hidden truth or enduring geographical reality to north, south, east and west, because such truth does not exist. Instead, it follows the 'paths' of each cardinal direction in different cultures through time. Embracing one set of directional language meanings rather than another shows that the nature of each of the four directions across history and between cultures is relative rather than absolute. When it comes to the words any of us use for these directions in whatever language, written and geographical context is vital. Situatedness is everything in understanding the cardinal directions.

While language and the 'family resemblances' between the four points are central to how we understand them, some cognitive psychologists believe that the mental grasp of direction may even have preceded language in early humans. Space was prior to language, hence spatial words and metaphors became central to linguistic development and evolution.[3] As well as 'up' and 'down', innumerable spatial terms suffuse ancient and modern languages, characterizing conceptual systems and personal relationships. They range from 'close friends' and 'growing apart' to 'the end of the road' and 'putting it all behind you'.[4]

In the English language, to 'orient' yourself is to locate yourself in space, yet the word comes from the Latin *oriens*, meaning 'east' or 'rising' (as in the Sun). The literal meaning of 'disorientation' is to lose sense of the direction of the east. From here ideas and beliefs quickly multiply and overlap, depending on the rules or language games we inhabit. Thanks to the prevailing mapping system developed in Europe we 'orient' ourselves vertically by imagining north is up – as in the phrase to go 'up north' – in contrast to going 'down south'.

For many societies the north is also a place of negative associations of cold and darkness, yet in different times and places where the rules of its use operate differently it can also have positive connotations of wonder and constancy. The south is often associated with warmth and light, yet in other contexts it can be a byword for indolence and under-development. To 'go west', popularly associated with modernity and the apprehension of 'frontiers', especially in North America, has also been synonymous with death and entering the afterlife through the twilight and the descent into night in following an arc from one horizon to the other. Such associations of mortality with the west mean that no cultures have enduringly placed west at the top of their maps as a cardinal direction, whereas all three other directions have been used at the top of world maps at various times by different cultures.

Virtually all human societies use language and writing to identify the four cardinal directions in naming and positioning themselves and their members in relation to the wider world. Initially, the four directions are described as things – winds, people, spirits – that are exterior and come towards us. Over time these descriptions and their meanings change as travel – driven by migration, trade or war – meant people went *towards* a specific point labelled north or south, east or west. Such points became increasingly important for those who left their communities to travel and navigate to places beyond the horizon, alongside other signs such as landmarks, sounds and smell. As human mobility increased so did the lexicon of the cardinal directions, which took on more abstract meanings and associations as people spread out across the globe. They were no longer aided by simple directional terms with tangible local significance such as 'up' and 'down', as used originally by people like the Manus islanders of Papua New Guinea in describing their proximity to sea and land, or 'left' and 'right', which in Hawaiian (*'Ōlelo Hawai'i*) equate to south (*Hema*) and north (*Akau*). Instead, north, south, east or west became fixed geometrical directions to follow. Their evolving terms provided etymologies for many of the cardinal directions in modern vernacular languages.

The four directions are not just directions – they have been fundamental to the cosmological views, morals, religious life and political economy of societies around the world. They described the reading of the movement of the heavens, they were used to determine the direction of prayer and they designated the sites and orientation of places of worship. They also came to influence how we organize and divide the world geopolitically into East and West (or Orient and Occident), the underdeveloped 'Global South' and the industrialized 'developed North'. As a result, they even contribute to assumptions and beliefs about who we are. I am recognized as and identify myself as a 'northerner', born in Bradford in Yorkshire, where I grew up in the 1970s before leaving to live in the south of England in the late 1980s, never to return for any length of time. Yet I identify with many of the clichéd traits of northerners and the north. Depending on where I am and where I speak, it can mean I come from a freezing, desolate, post-industrial wasteland full of whippets and bad food, or at another point a place of tough love, warmth, tight-knit communities and good beer. When I identify as 'northern', I am using a set of meanings for 'north' different from those involved in navigation or expressing orientation, which involve different language rules. Not all four cardinal directions attract such powerful personal identifications. Although people often classify themselves with some pride as 'northerners' or 'southerners' in the UK, few call themselves 'easterners'. In a global sense – a different category of the language game – to be labelled 'Oriental' has a long and undistinguished history. Once an indicator of assumed superiority, to be described as a westerner can now be pejorative.

As much as the four directions have allowed people to understand themselves in contrast to others, they have also enabled whole communities to locate themselves in the wider world. They are what linguists would call an 'object abstraction', where terms are used for concepts that develop far beyond the objects – or directions – to which they were first related. Early societies used the four nouns – east, west, north and south – to understand and by extension impose order on the vast and potentially limitless terrestrial and celestial space that surrounded them. In classical Greek and early European astronomy the North and South Poles were purely imaginative projections. They envisaged the Earth as the still point at the centre of the universe, with a giant axis running from the Pole Star seen high in the sky right through the poles and the middle of the Earth which lay at the centre of the cosmos. There is nothing physically tangible about the poles (nor the Equator, or prime median) as geographical places like islands or mountains: calculating their exact positions is subject to fluctuation and they are as much metaphorical as scientific, but they have become embedded in the language and imagination of many people as defining these two cardinal directions. It is this imaginative dimension of all four cardinal directions that means the story told here is composed of fiction and poetry as well as science, geography and history.

So why have so many societies chosen four directions, and why do they prioritize one as a prime direction over the others? NASA resolved their problem of an 'upside-down' image of the planet by inverting it to assert the fundamental righteousness of the understanding of the world with north at the top. But there is no fundamental and 'correct' orientation. So why not use two or five instead of four directions, and why place north at the top of our world maps? These questions – and their answers – are the subject of the following chapters.

Humans are not alone in having a sense of the cardinal directions to find their way home and avoid getting lost. Many zoologists now believe that migrating animals are reliant on an internal 'map' using a complex 'navigational toolbox' that perceives direction as they move across the lines of the Earth's magnetic field, the movement of the Sun during the day and the pattern of the stars at night. The annual migrations of millions of birds, mammals and even insects like the monarch butterfly utilize this 'toolbox' – much of it still as yet unclear to scientists – that enables them to obtain information not dissimilar to that provided by a compass and travel thousands of kilometres every year to eat, reproduce and still find their way back to where they first began. Studies have discovered traces of magnetite – an iron-oxide mineral with magnetic properties – in the beaks of most migratory birds, as well as salmon, dolphins, frogs, turtles, bats and rodents, suggesting they may somehow use this magnetic attraction to navigate on a north–south axis. Whatever the exact nature of the tools used by animals to migrate, the Earth's geomagnetic field and the Sun's movement, which together gave rise to human terms for the cardinal directions, seem to play a role in their perpetual movement across the planet's surface.[5]

The Power of Four

Humans do not have an innate neurological toolbox like animals, but they do possess language. The configuration and language of the four directions is common to many – though not all – cultures. They probably even pre-dated astronomical observations of the Sun's movements and the stars and were first inspired by the 'egocentric coordinates' of the human body. Our most basic corporeal orientations are fourfold: front and back, left and right. In many ancient languages 'front' and 'back' are synonymous with east and west, while 'left' and 'right' are often equivalent to north and south. So in Hebrew, east – *qedem* or *mizrach* – also means 'forward' or 'front', while 'west' – *achor* – is a synonym for 'behind'. In Arabic, north is *al-shamāl* ('left'), south is *al-janūb* ('right'). For both these languages the universe, in which sacred and ritual beliefs are based on facing east, mirrors the body.

Other cultures use the body's position to interpret directions in very different ways. Many of the terms used are *deictic*, in other words they are dependent on their physical context and can shift according to the speaker's point of view (examples of deictic terms about space include 'here', 'there' and 'across'). In ancient Chinese, the pictograph for north, 北, or *běi*, represents two people back to back, the dark and cold north synonymous with the 'back' of the body, whose 'front' looks southwards (*nán*), in the direction of light and warmth. In Japanese, north is *kita* – 'behind' or 'afterwards' – with *minima* meaning south, a feminine version of 'to face'.[6]

Many south-eastern African Bantu languages also use corporeal references to distinguish between the four cardinal directions. In Kihehe, the language of the Hehe people of Tanzania, north is *kumitwe*, which derives from *mitwe*, or 'head', and south is *magulusiika*, from *magulu*, meaning leg.[7] Along similar

1. *Aduno kine*, or 'life of
the world', Dogon rock-art
painting, Mali

lines, ancient rock art made by the Dogon people of Mali often
depicted a personification of the 'life of the world', or *aduno kine*,
as a simple diagrammatic figure personifying the Dogon creation
myth in which the deity Amma stretched an egg-shaped ball of
clay in four directions with north at the top to create the world
grasped in the god's hands. Cave paintings show a figure with a
torso and arms forming a cross that represents the four cardinal
directions. The head is north, the legs south, the left arm east and
the right west.[8]

Dividing orientation into four directions emanating from
the body is part of a larger symbolic fascination with ordering
natural phenomena. In mathematics four is the smallest compos-
ite number (a number divisible by a number apart from one and
itself). In geometry it is related to the cross and the square and
their associations with totality and completeness. The Arabic
numeral 4 originated in a simple cross which added the diagonal
stroke that is now most familiar in Western numerals. Quadripartite symbolism has provided many cultures and religions with
an organizing principle for the seasons, continents, winds, elements, ages of 'man', natural causes (according to Aristotle) and
the four corners of the Earth.

The ancient Chinese dynasties divided their domains into
four lands (*si tu*) and imagined the world formed by four seas.
Each of the four cardinal directions were imagined as 'intelligent

12

creatures': the green dragon of the east; the crimson bird of the south; the white tiger of the west; and the black turtle of the north, each coloured direction matching the hues of the soil in the corresponding Chinese regions. Buddhism believes in the four cardinal directions representing elements and cycles in life, moving from east (dawn) through south (noon and fire), west (dusk and autumn) and north (night and dissolution). Hinduism reveres the four *Vedas* (religious texts) and alongside Hindu mythology includes the *Lokapāla*, the four guardians of the cardinal directions: *Indra* (east), *Yama* (south), *Varun'a* (west) and *Kubera* (north).

Winds of Change

The earliest surviving record of the four cardinal directions was made during the first great Mesopotamian empire, the Akkadian dynasty (*c.* 2350–2150 BCE), whose ruler Naram-Sin (*r. c.* 2254– 2218 BCE) is the first known to have adopted the title 'King of the Four Corners of the World'.[9] Archaeological excavations undertaken in 1931 at Yorgan Tepe, south-west of Kirkuk in modern Iraq, unearthed hundreds of clay tablets containing Akkadian and Sumerian cuneiform inscriptions. One of the most significant of them measures just under seven by eight centimetres. It is a topographical map and is usually referred to as the 'Gasur map' (Plate 2). At its centre is an agricultural estate, through which a river runs from top right to bottom left before branching off into two tributaries that flow into a larger body of water on the far left. The settlement sits in a valley with two mountain ranges running across the top and bottom of the map. The lake has recently been identified as Zrebar (or Zerivar) Lake in the Kurdistan province of western Iran. The inscriptions offer an account of the central agricultural estate, described as 300 hectares of 'cultivated land'.[10]

The Gasur map is the oldest known map to show and name cardinal directions. The damaged semi-circle top left is labelled *IM-kur*, 'east'; the one bottom left is inscribed *IM-mar-tu*, 'west'; and to the centre left *IM-mir*, 'north'. Presumably the missing section of the tablet's right-hand side originally included the inscription *IM-ulù*, 'south'. Yet the naming here is not quite what it seems. The prefix '*IM*' ('tumu') refers to winds – the map identifies four directions by meteorological experiences rather than astronomical observations. Other Mesopotamian texts describe four principal winds forming a diagonal cross, equivalent to the modern directions of north-west, north-east, south-east and south-west. These translate into the Akkadian terms on the Gasur map as *IM-kur*, a north-eastern 'mountain' wind, which blows in from the Zagros mountain range to the north-east of Mesopotamia; *IM-mart-tu*, a south-western 'desert' wind derived from the word *Amurru*, describing the nomadic Amorite people of Syria and Palestine west of the Euphrates, as well as the direction from which hot sandstorms blow; *IM-mir*, the most prevalent wind from the north, a regular, strong, yet dry wind that cools the land; and *IM-ulù*, a south-eastern 'demon' or 'cloud' wind that originates in the Persian Gulf, bringing un-predictable, gloomy and wet weather.[11]

These cardinal directions referred to quadrants rather than points and derived from specific aspects of human and physical geography. For the farmers cultivating the land in Azala (modern-day Kurdistan) over 4,000 years ago, the four cardinal directions in terms of prevailing winds were not only a means of orientation: understanding wind direction and changeable climatic conditions was crucial for the cultivation of crops and could mean the difference between feast and famine. When the cuneiform text on the map is read from top to bottom, *IM-mir*, the direction from which the regular north-western winds blow, is the prime orientation.

On the Gasur map, *IM-mir* is established as a word with connotations of fertility, renewal, prosperity and temperance, in contrast to *IM-ulù*, which operates within Akkadian social conventions and language as a term evoking volatility, danger and the fear of outsiders. At this stage in history, the connotations of these two directions became embedded in the rhythms of sedentary, agricultural societies with little or no reference to travel or orientation, which were largely irrelevant to such communities. The words and connotations of cardinal directions that are spoken give shape and order to societies; they are part of an activity that anchors people within their physical world and makes sense of their surroundings.

The Mesopotamian combination of meteorological, geographical and ethnological words for the four directions and their various connotations find parallels, albeit in very different terms and under contrasting conditions, across the globe and in many languages throughout early recorded history. The prevalence of other directions, such as egocentric references – those from a subjective perspective like front/back, left/right – and allocentric examples – using landmarks or objects including rivers and mountains independent of a subject's point of view – are greater in some languages. Indigenous cultures like that of the Guugu Yimithirr people in Queensland in Australia's far north have an acute sense of cardinal directions but with little perception of egocentric coordinates. Instead they use a system of 'absolute' geographical orientation, referring to things and places as relative to the cardinal directions, rather than themselves. Rather than saying, 'Please move to the left', they would say, 'Please move to the west', and 'Pass the salt, it's to the north', instead of 'Pass the salt, it's under your nose'.[12] Some – usually societies sparsely populating small regions, such as the Yurok people of northern California – possess no terms for any of the four directions. Compass points are common to most societies, but they are not universal.[13]

The etymologies of cardinal directions across different cultures reveal their speakers' preoccupations with and rules for using each word within any given society. In Africa the language games within which each direction found expression were often defined through complex ethnological distinctions. The Zulu word for south is *iningizimu*, which translates as 'many cannibals'. Traditionally the sea lay directly south of the Zulu kingdom, the origin of cold winds and fog that hid malevolent spirits and man-eating monsters. Various south-east African languages also derive the names of cardinal directions from neighbouring ethnic groups: the Setswana and Sesotho languages use *bokane* (north) to describe Nguni-speaking people to the north, while *borwa* (south) derives from the word for 'Bushmen', or the Khoisan of southern Africa.[14]

Ancient Mesoamerican cosmologies used cardinal directions to describe their gods and stories of Creation. The Mayans of northern central America understood east and west first, based on astronomical observations of the rising and setting Sun, before meanings associated with north and south.[15] In Mayan belief, their solar god and creator, *Itzamná*, split into four deities called the *Bacab* (sometimes shown as jaguars) that held up the four corners of the world, each one representing a direction and a colour. East (translated as 'exit' – of the Sun emerging from the underworld) was associated with red and fire, and west (translated as 'entrance' of the Sun setting into the underworld) with black, symbolizing darkness and imminent night. North (often associated with white) and south (usually labelled yellow) were less demarcated as both directions and colours, and changed over time and across Mesoamerican languages and cultures.

What was strikingly different about Mayan and subsequent Mesoamerican cardinal directions from those of Mesopotamia and most other cultures was that they operated on three, not two axes. The Aztecs imagined the Earth as a horizontal disk divided by the dual east–west and north–south axes. At its centre ran a third, vertical *axis mundi*. The result was a *quincunx*, a geometric pattern of five points arranged like a cross, effectively structuring the Aztec world picture according to *five* directions. In 1325 CE the Aztec city of Tenochtitlan (modern Mexico City) was founded around the Templo Mayor, which symbolized the Aztec centre of the world, where the vertical and horizontal axes of the cardinal directions met, and the heavens, the Earth and the underworld came together.

Greek philosophy and science showed no interest in a fifth direction, nor colour-coding the directions. Instead it inherited the Mesopotamian agricultural preoccupation with winds. Mythical personifications of the four directions as gods, or *Anemoi*, first appear in the ancient works of Homer (*c*. 800 BCE). His *Iliad* and *Odyssey* both mention four gods representing cardinal winds. *Boreas*, the north wind, is possibly an archaic variant of 'mountains' or 'roaring'; *Notos*, the south wind, derives from 'moist'; *Eurus*, the east wind, comes from the 'brightness' of sunrise; the western wind of *Zephyrus* stems from the 'gloom' of sunset.

In ancient Greece weather was assumed to emanate from Zeus, but his meteorology was fickle and unpredictable. Subsequent natural philosophy wanted to challenge the view that natural phenomena such as the weather lay in the hands of Zeus and other deities. As the rules of the game shifted so did the language of the four directions: astronomical observations began providing alternative names, including describing the north as *Arctos*, or 'the bear', taken from the northern constellation of Ursa Major.

The earliest and most powerful case for the centrality of climate and directions in Greek life was made by Aristotle in *Meteorology* (*c*. 350 BCE). Taking as his subject 'everything which happens naturally', Aristotle described the Earth as a sphere sitting at the centre of the universe. *Meteorology* included the

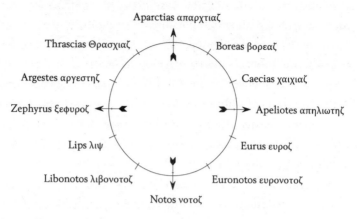

2. Timosthenes' twelve-point system of the winds, *c.* 270 BCE

earliest known geometrical diagram to codify cardinal directions according to wind systems, showing the northern hemisphere with Greece at the centre. It shows eight principal winds, or twelve altogether including 'half winds' (*Eurus* is replaced with *Apeliotes*, the 'heat of the sun'). This systematic codification of winds as coming *from* a specific direction was central to Aristotle's ethnological approach to the Earth, which he divided into five climatic – *klimata*, meaning 'slope' or 'incline' – zones. They were based partly on meteorological conditions, as Aristotle reasoned that the 'incline' of the Sun lessened the further north one travelled from the Equator, creating intemperate zones at the poles and the Equator, leaving just two habitable 'temperate' zones.

Greek agriculture and its growing maritime trade needed to anticipate the weather, as Aristotle's disciple Theophrastus of Eresos (*c.* 371–287 BCE) knew. In his book *On Winds* (*c.* 300 BCE), he claimed that 'what happens in the sky, in the air, on Earth and on the sea is due to the wind'.[16] Timosthenes of Rhodes (fl. 270 BCE) went even further. His twelve wind directions each described different regions and people. This was a significant development in human geography that subsequently connected cardinal winds with geographical directions and cultures. *Aparctias* (north) was associated with Scythia, the Central Asian nomadic kingdom; *Notus* (south) with Ethiopia; *Apeliotes* (east) with Bactriana, covering most of Afghanistan; *Zephyrus* (west) with the Straits of Gibraltar, the westernmost limits of the classical world. Celtica, Iberia, India and others were also aligned with winds. As the preoccupations of Greek thinking embraced human geography and trade, so the words for each direction changed and the rules of their usage also shifted. This began a conflation of direction with identity that still persists today.

The Greeks even built a 'Tower of Winds' that still stands in Athens. Designed by the astronomer Andronicus of Cyrrhus around 100 BCE, each side of the octagonal tower shows deities facing one of eight principal directions: *Boreas* (north), *Apeliotes* (east), *Notus* (south), *Zephyrus* (west), as well as *Kaikas* (north-east), *Eurus* (south-east), *Lips* (south-west) and *Skiron* (north-west). Not only is the tower the first known weather station, it also functioned as one of the earliest known clock towers (*horologion*). Below each deity is a sundial; inside the tower are the remains of a water-clock, the beginnings of a long history in which the measurement of time is involved in understanding direction.

The Tower of the Winds stood in the Roman Agora (27–17 BCE), or meeting place, and the Romans gradually adopted the Greek terms for winds and introduced new Latin words. North came first, named *borealis* or *septentrionalis*, a reference to the 'seven stars' of Ursa Major. South was given several new terms, including *australis* ('harsh' or 'sharp') or *meridionalis* (from 'midday'). West was *occidentalis* ('falling' or 'passing away') and east was *orientalis* ('rising' or 'originating') or *subsolanus* (literally 'under the sun'). Nevertheless, the adaptation was messy and contradictory, with some Greek names being retained, competing

Latin synonyms introduced and debates about the correct number of wind directions. The Roman architect Vitruvius even introduced a twenty-four-point wind 'rose' in his book *On Architecture* (*c.* 30–15 BCE). Vitruvius emphasized the importance of harmony, order and proportion in planning 'the orientation of the streets and lanes according to the regions of the heavens' and the winds.[17] The Greek 'pneuma' means air in motion, understood as breath – or wind. The outside air, or wind, we breathe – from whatever direction – is what keeps us alive. The character and quality of winds determined life and death.

In later societies the winds were central to personal orientation. For the Inuit people living in the Arctic regions of Greenland, Canada and Alaska, the primary tools for navigation were the winds and snowdrifts, elements of a very different environment to that of the Greeks. Winds were personified and gendered according to their temperament. The north-western *Uangnaq* is often regarded as the prevailing wind and considered female, due to its volatile nature: it can gust furiously then die away just as quickly. The 'male' south-easterly *Nigiq* blows in more steadily and is believed to 'retaliate' to its opposite, the *Uangnaq*. This gendered pair formed a cardinal axis, with *Kanangnaq* (north-east) and *Akinnaq* (south-west) completing the four Inuit cardinal directions.[18]

Boxing the Compass

The most decisive moment within early post-classical European ideas of cardinal directions came in the early ninth century CE under Charlemagne (748–814), king of the Franks and emperor of much of the northern part of the continent. In attempting to unify central and western Europe he initiated many political, economic and educational reforms – including renaming the four directions using monosyllabic proto-Germanic words, all derived from Indo-European roots. The winds become irrelevant: instead, this new classification was based entirely on the Sun's movement. *Nord* (north) came from the proto-Indo-European term *nórto-s* – 'lower', or to the 'left' (of the rising Sun looking east). *Est* (east) drew on the Indo-European *austo-s* – 'light' or 'shine' (as in the morning), which was in turn taken from the Sanskrit *uṣas*, or dawn. *Sund* (south) derived from an archaic term for the Sun, *sú-n-to-s*, referring to the south as the direction of the midday Sun (in the northern hemisphere). *Oëst* (west) took its name from the proto-Indo-European *uestos* with its various meanings of the evening including red (as in the setting Sun).[19]

These proto-Germanic terms also influenced the Norse words for each direction which were developed following the ninth-century settlement of Iceland from Norway. Norse used basic directional adverbs to describe sailing *út* ('out') from Norway to Iceland, with the return voyage described as *útan*, 'from the place which is "out"'. With no knowledge of the compass, Norse navigators relied on watching the weather and wildlife and using the four senses to avoid what medieval sagas called *hafvilla*: losing course or direction at sea.[20] What emerged were the four directions: *austr* (east), *suðr* (south), *vestr* (west) and *norðr* (north), from which Norway, or *Norðvegr* – a sailing route along the country's coastline, meaning 'northern way' or 'northern route' – took its name.[21] Cognate versions of these terms *norðr, austr, suðr* and *vestr* came to predominate and are still recognizable in most modern European vernaculars, including the Romance languages. North is *norte* in Portuguese and Spanish, *nord* in French and Italian and *Norden* in German – although very few speakers of these languages are probably aware that the word comes from 'left' in relation to facing the rising Sun.

It was only in the twelfth century CE that references to the magnetic compass using this vernacular language started to appear in the Mediterranean – long after the invention of the first compasses in the second century BCE in China. The Chinese made *Si Nan*, pieces of magnetite fashioned into spoon-like shapes corresponding to the outline of Ursa Major, with a north–south axis that followed the Earth's natural forces.

Over time the Chinese developed iron needles rubbed with lodestones to magnetize them. The needles were then placed in water, allowing them to float and orient themselves on the magnetic north–south axis. Known as *tzhu-shih*, or 'loving stone', the Chinese used this apparently magical object in divination and geomancy (often called *Feng-shui*) to predict astrological phenomena and to site buildings on a north–south axis, aiming to unify individuals with their environment. The supreme example is the building of Beijing's iconic fifteenth-century Forbidden City, whose front gates and windows faced the Sun and warming winds from the south.

What was particularly striking about early Chinese compasses was their orientation: the Chinese called them *luojing*, translated as 'the thing that points south' (*zhinan*). (Plate 5) The tip of the magnetized needle pointed south, with the north–south axis usually indicated by a metal wire. The Chinese compass was one of the 'Four Great Inventions' of ancient China, along with gunpowder, paper and printing, first identified by Sir Francis Bacon in his *Novum Organum* (1620). These first compasses were made from lodestone, a word originating in Middle English for 'journey' or 'course'. A lodestone is a naturally magnetized piece of magnetite, like the iron oxide found in the heads of migrating animals, and is the most magnetic of the Earth's minerals. For the Greek philosopher Thales of Miletus (*c.* 624–546 BCE), the lodestone's ability to attract another piece of iron and magnetize it (a process known as induction) could only be explained by animism: the lodestone must possess a soul. What nobody understood until the nineteenth century was how the electrons in any mineral spin around the core of its atoms, generating an electric current and causing the electrons to act like magnets. When the electrons spin in the same direction in substances like iron, cobalt and nickel they become magnetic. They are magnetized once another magnetic substance enters their magnetic field. Since the twentieth century, scientists have argued that lodestones are magnetized when struck by lightning, whose powerful electromagnetic field causes all the magnetic domains in the lodestone to line up, creating magnetic force. All magnets have north and south poles, so any ferrous metals containing iron can be magnetized when rubbed with a lodestone, as their atoms line up in the same direction, the force of which creates a magnetic field. This is how the earliest compass needles were made.[22]

In medieval Europe magnetized needles primarily – though not exclusively – pointed north and were labelled accordingly. The reasons for the differences between the south-pointing Chinese compasses and north-pointing European ones are explained as the subsequent chapters follow the four points of the compass.

How the compass migrated, whether through traders moving along the Silk Road or because of a separate development, is unclear. Muslim scholars were describing Persian pilots using magnetic compasses in the Red Sea as early as the 1230s.[23] The first European descriptions are of 'dry' magnetic compasses in navigation, magnetized needles mounted on pivots and placed in boxes to orient the direction of travel by magnetic north (and by extension south). In his book *Of the Nature of Things* (*c.* 1190), the English theologian Alexander Neckam provided the first known European reference to the compass in navigation, writing that, when sailors 'sail over the sea, when in cloudy weather they can no longer profit by the light of the Sun, or when the world is wrapped up in the darkness of the shades of night, and they are ignorant to what point of the compass their ship's course is directed, they touch the magnet with a needle which is whirled round in a circle until, when its motion ceases, its point looks direct to the north'.[24] Neckam's comments show that using the compass was already part of navigational practice that privileged north as the main cardinal direction.

Neckam was also quick to find a moral and religious value to defining the north via astronomical observation. *Polaris*, the North Star, was also synonymous with the Virgin Mary and became known as 'Our Lady, Star of the Sea'. 'Behold the Pole Star!' he wrote, 'the apex of the north, shining out on high. The sailor at night directs his course by it, for it stands motionless at the fixed hinge of the turning sky – and Mary is like the Pole Star.'[25] Over the next century the term 'cardinal' would come to represent the four moral virtues of justice, prudence, temperance and fortitude, the seven sins and the three orders of cardinal (bishop, priest and deacon) in the Roman Catholic Church. These theological meanings of the term would from this point onwards coexist alongside its directional sense of 'principal' or 'fundamental' in relation to the four points of the horizon. Direction would now take on a more moral meaning than ever before.

In 1269 the French mathematician Petrus Peregrinus ('Peter the Wayfarer') wrote the *Epistola de magnete* ('Letter on the Magnet'), the first systematic scientific explanation of geomagnetism based on experiments with spherical lodestones. His was the first book to use the term 'poles' in describing how to understand dipolarity by identifying north and south on a lodestone, explaining that 'these two points will be diametrically opposite, like the poles of a sphere'.[26] He understood magnetic attraction and repulsion through the use of the term 'polarity', showing through simple experimentation that 'the north pole of one lodestone attracts the south pole of another, while the south pole attracts the north'. His ground-breaking experiments also revealed that 'unlike' poles attract, whereas 'like' poles repel each other. He realized that breaking a lodestone in half 'did not destroy the properties of the parts of the stone, since it is homogenous', and simply created two smaller magnets with unchanged magnetic poles (the composition of magnets remains the same down to the atomic level, however small you divide them).[27] Peregrinus understood that magnetism was somehow derived from the Earth itself, which lay at the centre of the universe, and so 'from the poles of the world, the poles of the lodestone receive their virtue', and not, as Neckam believed, from the stars, including *Polaris*.[28]

Petrus's explanation of magnetism and how to make compasses for use in seaborne navigation led to the development of a new genre of maritime maps called portolans or 'compass charts'. These were drawn using compass measurements and even included compass roses (sometimes also called 'wind roses', which are more precisely where lines of navigational bearing intersected). They refined the classical models of Aristotle and others using a new language for directions based on geography and the polyglot *lingua franca* of Mediterranean maritime life in Greek, Latin, Arabic and Catalan. An eight-wind system evolved based on the four cardinal directions. They were *Tramontana* (north), from the Latin for 'across the mountains' – an explicit reference to the Alps, with the added dimension of referring to anything 'foreign' or 'barbaric'. *Levante* (east) came from the Latin for 'rising' (of the Sun). *Ostro* (south) derived from the Latin 'auster', hot and humid winds. *Ponente* (west) came from mixed Latin, Italian and Catalan terms for 'setting' (Sun) and mild, westerly breezes. The other four winds given individual names drew on various languages and geographical regions: south-west was called either *Garbino* – an Arab word – or *Libeccio*, meaning Libya (associated with Africa in general); north-east was *Greco*, or Greece; south-east was *Sirocco* (also spelled *Scirocco*), an Arab-Italian term for a hot, rising wind; north-west was *Mistral*, taken from the Latin for 'masterful' or 'dominant'.

The properties of the magnetic compass meant that in most societies it pointed north (with the exception of China), but by the time European navigators were using it in the twelfth century many cultures had a prearranged astronomical and meteorological grid – or more accurately circle – within which to accommodate it, along with the other cardinal directions. The compass fitted into well-established conventions for understanding the four cardinal directions, rather than vice versa.

By the fifteenth century the use of the compass led to the refinement of compass roses on maps showing thirty-two different directions composed of four cardinal directions, eight principal winds, eight half-winds and sixteen quarter-winds. It established the basic connection between compass points and navigation, a term compounded from the Latin *navis* ('ship') and *agere* ('act', or 'drive'). In a more sophisticated form these connections remain in place in maritime sailing today, understood primarily through European beliefs about direction and orientation.

Prior to the use of compasses in navigation, establishing north could involve using the midday Sun (identifying south and in direct contrast, north) or *Polaris*, the North Star, but these were also approximate calculations that left any notion of a precise and verifiable point of 'absolute north' impossible. Such astronomical methods for establishing absolute direction came with its own problems. Gravitational force upon the Earth causes it to 'wobble' slightly as it rotates on its axis, a process known as 'precession'. As a result, *Polaris* is not always exactly due north of the North Pole (although at this point in time their alignment is quite close). In thousands of years' time precession will mean that other stars in nearby constellations could function more accurately as the North Star. In fact, *Polaris* was not used in any way accurately as the Pole Star until around 1300 CE.

By the seventeenth century the compass had become established in Europe as 'justly ranked amongst the greatest wonders that this world affords'.[29] However, by this time sailors and pilots had also identified a problem with the use of the magnetic compass in long-distance seaborne travel: there was not one 'true' north, but another 'magnetic' north, and the angle between the two is called 'declination' (or 'variation'). 'True north' – sometimes also called 'geographic north' – is the direction along the Earth's surface ending at a fixed point where the imaginary rotational axis of the planetary poles intersects its surface. It is where lines of longitude converge, marking the north and south poles. But a magnetic compass does not point to 'true north' (or 'true south'). Instead, it aligns itself with the planet's magnetic field and points to 'magnetic north' (and, by extension, 'true south'). Magnetic poles are located where the magnetic lines of attraction enter the Earth. As the north-seeking end of a magnet is attracted to its opposite, the south-seeking end (and repelled by its like end), then all magnetized compasses point 'north' to what is called the geographic North Pole, but which is actually a magnetic south pole. The term for 'north' was too well established to be changed by those using the compass, even though technically when it comes to the magnetic poles, north is south – and vice versa.[30]

The Earth's geomagnetic field also changes over time and depending on where you are on the planet. The fluid motion of molten iron and nickel in the Earth's outer core creates volatile electric currents, known as convection, that over billions of years turned the Earth into a giant 'geodynamic' magnet. Its magnetic field radiates outwards from the core into space, protecting the planet from destruction by radiation and charged particles; the magnetic lines of attraction then loop back and enter the Earth at the magnetic poles where the field is strongest. The English scientist William Gilbert (c. 1544–1603) was the first European to begin to understand magnetism in this way in his book *De Magnete* ('On the Magnet'), published in 1600.

Subtitled 'the Great Magnet the Earth', Gilbert proposed that 'our common mother (the earth)' was composed of a solid iron core – or bar – that caused magnetic repulsion and attraction.[31]

Unfortunately for early navigators and scientists like Gilbert attempting to identify some consistency to magnetism, the dynamic nature of the elements in the Earth's core means that its magnetic field is never stable. The magnetic poles are also not technically points of attraction where absolute north or south can be pinpointed: they are shifting approximations of where the magnetic field lines arise from the volatile compound magnetic forces at the Earth's centre that emerge perpendicular to its surface. A magnetized needle is trying to point inwards towards the Earth, rather than an external point on its surface. Taking a bearing of magnetic north or south can vary from 'true north' or 'true south' by hundreds of kilometres. Magnetic north was first established as situated in northern Canada's Nunavut territories by James Clark Ross in June 1831. Since then the planet's convection currents have seen magnetic north 'drift' several hundred kilometres from 'true north'. It is now located on Ellesmere Island, 600 kilometres from geographic north. This 'wandering pole' continues to move north-east around 15 kilometres a year, and is destined to end up in Siberia.

Even more confusing for scientists like Gilbert was the realization that declination led to magnetic variation across the Earth's surace, which is due to the shifting geomagnetic intensity of the Earth's molten core. Navigators had sensed the problem for generations, but it was only on long-distance ocean voyages that it became significant. At any given time a magnetic compass reading could be out by 'declination' of over 20 degrees, which on a trans-oceanic voyage of thousands of kilometres was a margin of error that could prove disastrous. On his first voyage to the Americas in 1492, Columbus realized that this magnetic variation also varied according to longitude. His diary regularly described

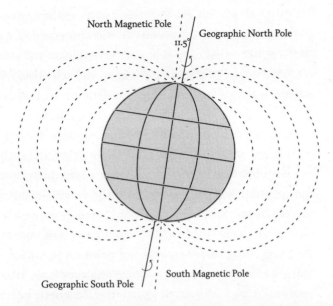

3. The Earth's Magnetic Field: the Geographic (or 'True') north is a fixed point on a map based on the Earth's rotation axis. Magnetic north is the direction a compass points in aligning itself with the Earth's magnetic field which is constantly changing. The difference between the two points is on average 11.5 degrees.

how, on his compasses, 'the needle deviated to the north-west', requiring approximate compensation using guesswork as much as anything else.[32] Edmund Halley's 1701 map of magnetic declination or variation in the Atlantic Ocean (Plate 7) was just the first of many attempts to measure geomagnetic variation – which also became known as 'inclination' around the world.[33]

Both astronomical precession and magnetic declination can now be calculated with a high degree of mathematical accuracy. Small magnets and iron compensators can be used to offset a compass's magnetic variation, and pilots can refer to world magnetic variation charts to calculate direction between true and magnetic bearings using the acronym CADET – 'Compass ADd East for True' – involving the addition or subtraction of an eastern bearing. But for thousands of years they were subject to highly subjective and localized interpretation. That local subjectivity, which makes the four points of the compass so evocative for artists and writers, also makes them challenging for scientists and navigators.

*

Which direction comes first? From the Greco-Roman world Europe inherited then exported the assumption that the points of the compass are always paired as opposites – north–south, east–west – and in the English language-speaking world there is an assumption that they should be described according to each axis. Yet they are also read clockwise starting in the north then moving from east to south and west. This is not, however, a universally accepted belief. The primacy of the south in China's orientation of the compass points seems to have established a different order running clockwise – east, south, west, north. This book's four chapters follow yet another trajectory, one that charts the diurnal passage of time, tracing the Sun's arc throughout the day. It therefore starts as the Sun rises in the morning in the east (chapter 1), often the first direction identified by early societies as the beginning of light, warmth and life. As the Sun passes through the zenith at midday it is possible to identify due south (chapter 2) and its opposite, due north (chapter 3), before we finally conclude as the Sun sets in the west (chapter 4).

In showing how cardinal directions have been understood in different ways by various societies in language through time, the book reveals how they do more than simply enable orientation and navigation – important though that is. They are central to our language, naming and fixing our personal identities. They also play a part in naming states and places, such as South Africa, East Timor, Northern Ireland, Western Sahara and that most contentious of regions, the 'Middle East', which can only be 'Middle' if the speaker presupposes an imagined geography that also includes a 'Near East' and a 'Far East' all in contrast with a binary opposite of 'West' and a centre in Europe. Many of these places possess deeply troubled histories, partly because of their naming via an apparently neutral compass point related to a sacred or political centre. Every prime direction is dictated by a fulcrum that privileges one direction over another, for religious or political reasons. In classical Greece the centre was Delos, the birthplace of Apollo, positioned between north and west. In medieval Christianity Jerusalem stood at the centre and east at the top, based on biblical stories of Creation and Christ's crucifixion. Early Muslim map-makers put south at the top with Mecca as their sacred centre. In the nineteenth century the British Empire placed London – specifically Greenwich – at the heart of a political map of space and time that put north at the top.

Today, online map applications tell us wherever we are in a specific moment through a mobile device guiding us through space, regardless of north and south, east or west. We simply want to get to where we are going as quickly and directly as we can. Fewer of us know any more how to find north and south, east and west, simply by looking into the sky or using a compass. What is the cost to who we are if we lose our sense of where we are?

EAST

Here Comes the Sun

In the story of cardinal directions, time and place start in the east. Naming 'east' establishes a rule for understanding it as the primal direction, the point of origin from which everything else unfolds. For millennia, the east has been an emblem of the human life cycle: the symbol of birth and the beginning of life's journey encapsulated in one day. The day ends with the setting of the Sun in the west bringing twilight and death. Unlike the north–south axis characterized by the belief in the physical place of the poles, the east–west one is marked by the diurnal passage of time from sunrise to sunset. For prehistoric societies the rising of the Sun in the east brought light, heat and hope. Many ancient cultures – Mesopotamia, Persia, Egypt, India and China – celebrated the east with its connotations of the beginning of life. Over time, the European world and its extension in North America cast the east as synonymous with all of these societies, in a political attempt to marginalize them as no longer at the centre of the world but on its eastern periphery. By the nineteenth century the East became a byword in the English-speaking world as a faraway place desired for its exoticism, luxury and wealth, but denigrated for its supposed barbarism and despotism, and populated by people stereotyped as dirty, lazy and licentious. Today the connotations of 'east' are shifting yet again, with the development of Asian economic power in the second half of the twentieth century in Japan, South Korea, China and

India. The global geopolitical and economic focus is returning once more to that area of the globe stretching from China to the Mediterranean, as the east shifts and changes more than any of the other cardinal directions.

Reverence for the east originates in ancient Sun worship among polytheistic religions, where a deity is often described as riding across the sky from east to west in a boat or chariot. They included the ancient Egyptian Sun god Ra, believed to rule over the world as king of the gods. Ancient Inca culture worshipped Inti or Apu-punchau, a Sun god fashioned out of gold. The Aztecs regarded themselves as 'people of the Sun', having lived through one of four 'Suns', or ages created then destroyed by their gods' struggle for control of the Sun. This led to the current era of the 'fifth Sun', created when the gods asked a mortal called Nana-huatzin to sacrifice himself by jumping into fire to ensure the Sun's regeneration. His sacrificial self-immolation allows him to arise as a flaming red Sun in the east. Only the endless repetition of this first blood sacrifice through ritualized slaughter would guarantee that the life-giving Sun reappeared to ensure life on Earth. In Hinduism, Surya (from the Sanskrit for 'Sun') is the solar deity and creator of the universe, depicted riding a chariot and expelling darkness. The Chinese late Shang Dynasty (c. 1200–1045 BCE) worshipped the Sun, to which they made sacrificial offerings, recorded on some of the earliest written records found in East Asia – oracle-bone inscriptions, carved on cattle or turtle bones and shells including those dedicated 'to the rising and setting Sun'.[1] As the Egyptians worshipped Ra as the Sun god, so in turn the Greeks and Romans created Apollo (also Phoebus in Roman) as their solar deity.

Such reverence for the Sun and the eastern horizon gradually developed more sophisticated social and moral meanings associated with the passage of time. The ancient Chinese character representing east, or dōng – 東 – depicts the Sun rising behind

a tree. The east became associated with the seasons and especially spring, wood (one of the five elements) and the colour
green; it could also connote the beginning of a day, a year, even a
life. Farming in the spring was known as 'eastern activities', with
the warm, damp winds from the east heralding the new season.
In following the seasons clockwise, classical Chinese culture
developed a different circular direction for the cardinal directions, starting with east (spring), then moving south (summer),
west (autumn) and ending in the north (winter). Following this
ESWN pattern, the Chinese spoke of 'east-south' and 'west-
north' in direct contrast to the Greco-Roman and European
ordinal (or intercardinal) directions.[2]

Yet, as in so many other classical cultures, the prime axis in
ancient China remained east–west based on the movement of
the Sun and the seasons. The Japanese word for 'east' is *higashi* –
東 – derived from *himukashi*, 'facing the Sun' and 'rising'.[3] The
Chinese word for 'thing' is *dōngxi*, literally 'east–west'; in other
words, anything that exists between east and west. But this
primary axis was subsequently qualified by a more political orientation. In the Chinese cosmological realm 'ziwei' is the Pole Star,
the residence of the celestial Ziwei Emperor, the 'Great Emperor
of the North Star'. The Chinese emperor was the 'Son of Heaven',
the earthly manifestation of the supreme deity inhabiting the
Pole Star. The emperor looked 'down' south on his subjects from
an elevated position on high in the north: everything to his left
was superior to what was on his right. But when his subjects
imagined directions, the reverse was the case: as they looked 'up'
north, east was the preferred symbolic direction on the right, and
west, to the left, its inferior. To be on the 'right' or eastern side
conferred privileged social status in various imperial, ceremonial
and domestic situations. East was also synonymous with 'host',
the west with the guest. *Yǒu xìng*, or 'right surnames', referred to
aristocratic or high-ranking families, and the expression 'no one

is on his right' meant that the individual being described had no superior. In contrast, the Chinese phrase, 'the left side of the street', is equivalent to the Anglo-American expression 'the wrong side of the tracks'.[4]

Monotheistic religions such as Judaism and Christianity tried to distance themselves from what they regarded as the idolatrous worship of the Sun and related Greco-Roman gods like Apollo and Heracles/Hercules in favour of one deity. But they still inherited a presumption of Creation's origins in the Sun and the east. This led to some contradictory approaches to the sacredness – or profanity – of particular directions. The theology of monotheism meant that the east soon became caught in a shifting language game between condemning the direction of Sun worship as negative, while defining its role in Creation as positive. For instance, the Essenes, a mystical Jewish sect that flourished from the second century BCE to the first century CE, observed the Torah of Moses but also prayed to their messiah as 'the great luminary', 'beseeching him to rise' in the east, in the language of Sun worship.[5]

Orthodox Jewish belief literally turned away from such explicit solar veneration. In the Old Testament Book of Ezekiel, the prophet, exiled in Babylon, describes idolatrous worship in the temple in Jerusalem. God shows Ezekiel religious 'abominations', including people 'with their backs toward the temple of the Lord, and their faces toward the east; and they worshipped the Sun toward the east' (Ezekiel 8:16).[6] In this geo-theology, worshipping the Sun was a sin that angered God as a hangover of pagan heliolatry that misunderstood the true theological significance of the east as the site of the Christian Creation and the direction of Christ's Second Coming.

For Jews and Christians, the east was central to the beginning and the end of times. But it would prove hard to reconcile theological time with an understanding of the four cardinal directions, because assuming a vertical passage from the beginning of life starting in the east, and ending in the west, also needed to assimilate the notion of heaven as 'up' and hell as 'down'. The story begins in Genesis: God 'planted a garden eastward in Eden' (Genesis 2:8), and after the Fall Adam and Eve are also exiled to the east, from where the story of postlapsarian human history begins. Although Sun-worshipping was abominated, the Book of Ezekiel nevertheless conceded that 'the god of Israel came by the way of the east' (Ezekiel 43:2). The time of the Messiah's Second Coming is predicted as coming from the east: 'For as the lightning cometh out of the east, and shineth even unto the west; so shall also the coming of the Son of Man be' (Matthew 24:27). In trying to supplant Sun worship, Judaism replaced the Sun with a city and reoriented its religious practice around Jerusalem and its holy sites. The faithful were told to 'pray to the Lord toward the city which you have chosen' (1 Kings 8:44). *Mizrach*, or east, thus became the Jewish direction of prayer. The diaspora would pray towards Israel wherever their location. When in Israel they faced Jerusalem, and if they lived in the holy city they prayed towards the Temple Mount. *Mizrach* became the term both for the wall in a synagogue that faced east, as well as a plaque in the home to indicate the direction of prayer.

Early Christianity expanded the Jewish *mizrach* by developing the Latin term *ad orientem* – 'to the east' – to understand east as its sacred cardinal direction. 'Orient' became the term for east in Latin-speaking Christendom from the second century CE. The early Church Fathers and official writings that prescribed orthodox theology and practice known as the Christian Apostolic Constitutions (*c.* 380 CE) repeatedly emphasized the importance of the east to Christian belief. As the location of the Garden of Eden, the east was also believed to be the direction from which Christ would also come towards Jerusalem at the time of the Second Coming. The faithful were urged to rise up with one consent, and looking towards the east ... pray to God eastward, who ascended up to the heaven of heavens to the east; remembering also the ancient situation of paradise in the east, from whence the first man, when he had yielded to the persuasion of the serpent, and disobeyed the command of God, was expelled.[7]

Christian groups praying at home faced east: beyond identifying the direction by pointing towards and naming it, the devotee physically genuflected towards the east, sometimes called 'Christi figura' in early churches – the direction a literal embodiment of Christ.[8] As the faith developed, churches were built according to this same eastward prescription. Jewish synagogues had a similar ethos, although oriented so their congregations faced Jerusalem, wherever they were in the world, which meant the synagogue's orientation was not always necessarily eastern. Similarly, mosques were required to face the Kaaba, a stone building at the centre of Islam's holiest site, the Masjid al-Haram in Mecca, whatever its direction relative to the location of the worshipper. In Christian churches the altar and by extension the celebrant and congregation were designed to face the east, the direction of Paradise. All of faith was 'oriented' according to the east. It followed that 'disorientation', for an early Christian, was not simply a loss of the east or even a loss of direction more generally, but an uncertainty as to where the truth lay.

The role of eastern liturgical orientation remained a feature of all subsequent Christian theology. The sixteenth-century English Reformation led the reformed Church of England literally to turn its back on the Catholic practice of *ad orientem* by having the clergy stand at the north end of the communion table and facing westward towards the congregation. But more traditional believers retained the early church practice whereby the priest stood behind the altar facing east. By the nineteenth century the controversy even reached Parliament and required legislation. The 'Oxford Movement' of High Anglicans during the 1830s and 1840s resurrected *ad orientem* during Communion, leading to such an uproar among the faithful that it was eventually banned by the Public Worship Regulation Act (1874). To advocate *ad orientem* remains a touchstone of traditional Catholic belief. In 2009 the conservative Pope Benedict XVI publicly celebrated Mass in the Vatican *ad orientem*. He explained his position in *The Spirit of the Liturgy* (2000), where he argued that 'a common turning to the east during the Eucharistic Prayer remains essential.' For Benedict this was a return to the basic principles of the Church, because 'praying towards the east is a tradition that goes back to the beginning. Moreover, it is a fundamental expression of the Christian synthesis of cosmos and history.' *Ad orientem* was both theological and architectural: 'we should definitely take up again the apostolic tradition of facing the east, both in the building of churches and in the celebration of the liturgy.'[9]

Turning East

Pope Benedict was certainly correct that the tradition of *ad orientem* went right back to the earliest Christian world views. One of the most powerful surviving visual examples is the mosaic map (*c.* 560 CE) that can be seen today on the floor of St George's Church in Madaba, central Jordan (Plate 8). Only a quarter of the original survives, but it remains one of the earliest depictions of the biblical lands, stretching from the Jordan Valley at the top to the Canopic branch of the Nile at the bottom. It is one of the first known maps oriented with east at the top and Jerusalem at its centre.

The sacred direction embedded in the Madaba mosaic was given greater theological depth in later Christian medieval world maps, or *mappae-mundi*, but which also faced the problem of how to relate four directions to a theology that concentrated on a vertical story of life and death, heaven and hell. When, in his *Dialogue on the Sacraments*, the twelfth-century theologian Hugh of St Victor is asked by one of his students, 'Where is paradise?', he points to a world map and says, 'Why do you ask what you can see? You begin in the east; what you see here is the Tree of Life.'[10] According to Hugh, Creation happened in the east – *in oriente* in Latin – and in a specific place shown on medieval Christian maps: the biblical Garden of Eden. Both terms originate from even older Semitic languages: 'garden' comes from the ancient Iranian word for 'paradise' (*pairidaēza*), which then entered Greek and Hebrew, while 'Eden' can be traced back to the Akkadian word for 'plain' and the Hebrew for 'pleasure'.

Hugh of St Victor compared the Earth to Noah's Ark, a symbol of the Church and its teachings. In his religious topography the four cardinal directions took on deeply moral meanings: 'the front of the Ark faces the east, and the rear faces the west . . . to the west is the Last Judgement . . . in the northern corner of this apex is hell.'[11] South took on various worldly associations. Hugh related it to Egypt, south of Jerusalem, the domain of heat, theological darkness and 'carnal concupiscence'. But the enduring prime axis remained east–west in Hugh's combination of theology and geography. According to his theography, 'what was brought about at the beginning of time would also have been brought about in the east – at the beginning of the world'.[12] Then, 'as time proceeded towards its end, the centre of events would have shifted to the west, so that we may recognise out of this that the world nears its end in time as the course of events has already reached the extremity of the world in space'.[13] All of biblical history ran in a vertical line from east at the top down to the furthest point known in the west, where time ends with the Resurrection. But this axis did not easily map onto the

Christian geography of heaven as 'up' and hell as 'down'. Hell was positioned by Hugh in the 'northern corner', while heaven was outside earthly time and space.

The difficulty in unifying Christian visions like Hugh's with the four cardinal directions can be seen in virtually all surviving medieval Christian world maps. The finest example, dated around 1300, is on display in Hereford Cathedral. On the Hereford *mappa-mundi* (Plate 10) the cardinal directions are represented on its outer ring from the top, moving clockwise, from *Oriens* (east), *Meridiens* (south), *Occidens* (west) to *Septentrio* (north, from the Latin for seven, referring to the seven stars of the Plough in Ursa Major, or the Great Bear). The Garden of Eden is shown at the top of the map, then time flows downwards through images of Old Testament empires, the birth of Christ and the rise of Rome, with Jerusalem at the centre. It ends at the westernmost point of Gibraltar at the bottom of the map, labelled the 'Columns of Hercules', the classical end of the world, and for Christianity the prefiguration of the Last Judgement. The northern (left) and southern (right) points on the map depict various geographical and theological extremities. The 'intolerable cold' of the north was contrasted with the far south, where the distended coastline of Africa portrays increasingly monstrous people and fantastic creatures deformed by what was believed to be the intemperate heat of the region.

Like all surviving medieval *mappae-mundi*, the Hereford map shows time as well as space. East is enthroned as the cardinal direction at its summit, from where the eye travels down to the west, and Judgement awaits at the end of time. Outside the terrestrial world, on the map's borders, Earthly time ends, replaced by the eternal present of Heaven, where there is no need for cardinal directions. And in the bottom corner of the *mappa-mundi* there is a figure on horseback, riding out of the frame, looking back at the world he is leaving. His expression is hard to determine;

the inscription above him reads, 'Continue on'. He seems to be exiting this sinful life. But, as he goes, he gazes wistfully back up to the cardinal direction of the east, perhaps remembering the rising of the Sun, the location from which all life begins, and the place of rebirth and renewal.

The quadripartite divisions shown on the Hereford *mappamundi* further clarified medieval Christian belief. They ranged from the four continents – Europe, Asia, Africa and a fourth antipodean region (from the Greek *antipodes*, to have one's feet in the opposite direction) – to the four corners of the Earth described in the Books of Isaiah and Revelation, the rivers of Paradise (Pishon, Tigris, Gihon and Euphrates), the Church Fathers (Ambrose, Jerome, Augustine and Gregory) and the Evangelists (Matthew, Mark, Luke and John) and their Four Gospels. Each continent, region, river, evangelist and book was given its own cardinal direction.

The Old Testament inherited dualistic beliefs – two fundamentally different yet complementary ideas – from earlier polytheistic and classical religions. This meant that the four directions took on contradictory associations depending on the context. East was both revered as a sacred direction but at other moments regarded with fear and suspicion as a place of wilderness, destructive winds and dangerous seas. Older connotations of the four directions evoking wind, weather and migration still remained influential and could affect theological language. In the Book of Ezekiel the downfall of the merchants of Tyre is caused by 'the east wind' that 'broke you in the midst of the seas' (Ezekiel 27:26). Heading eastwards is also the result of punishment and exile: it is where Adam and Eve are banished, as well as Lot (Genesis 13:11) and the children of Abraham's concubines (Genesis 25:6). The west was associated with Resurrection, but also with evil, death and darkness (Psalms, 104:19–20). Similarly, Jeremiah described how from the north 'an evil shall break forth upon all the inhabitants of the land' (Jeremiah 1:14), while the south was described as a 'land of trouble of anguish' (Isaiah 30:6). In the Book of Isaiah the north is explicitly linked with Satan, who claims, 'I will ascend into heaven, I will exalt my throne above the stars of God: I will sit also upon the mount of the congregation, in the sides of the north' (Isaiah 14:13). These beliefs were based on the assumption that temptation and evil could appear from any and every point, but God's grace and salvation could be found anywhere in the four corners of the world. It was a comprehensive approach that belied the difficulties of aligning the story of Christianity from Creation to Judgement Day with the four cardinal directions.

As Christianity tried to tell itself a convincing story about the east as the site of Creation – and the west as a place of Resurrection – early Islamic thought inherited and adapted its own beliefs in the theological power of the east. Like Judaism and Christianity, it also turned away from Sun worship of the kind practised by the south Arabian sects like the Sabaeans. The Koran explicitly forbade veneration of the stars or planets and required prayer times outside sunrise, noon or sunset, to avoid any suggestions that the faithful were worshipping the Sun. The expansion of Islam into northern then western Africa from the seventh century CE affected the *qibla*, the direction to which all Muslims are required to pray. *Qibla*, meaning 'which is opposite' in Arabic, was during the prophet Muhammad's lifetime associated with Jerusalem, towards which most early Muslim communities prayed. But in the second Hijri year (623 CE) the Kaaba – believed to have been built by Abraham (Ibrahim) and Ishmael (Ismail) – in Mecca was announced as the sacred direction of prayer. Muslims were subsequently instructed: 'Turn your face toward the Sacred Mosque [*al-Masjid al-Haram*]. And wherever you are, turn your faces toward it' (Koran 2:144).[14] This change in the direction of prayer from Jerusalem to Mecca and the Kaaba in particular was a crucial moment in creating a Muslim identity distinct from Judaism and Christianity: more than any other monotheistic religion, in the case of Islam, direction shaped belief. From this point onwards the *qibla* was increasingly set on an east–west axis as a result of Muslim conversions westwards throughout Africa and beyond. The *hadith* (the reported sayings of the Prophet Muhammad) also said that 'What is between the east and west is *qibla*.'[15] This affected languages across the continent. In the Saharan regions of southern Algeria the Kel Ahaggar people of the Muslim Tuareg confederation used the term *elkablet*, or 'the direction of Mecca', for east, which was also known as *dat-akal*, or 'the country in front' of those praying.[16]

Even as Christianity and Islam worked out their theology of the four directions, a newer method of orientation was beginning to emerge that qualified the more theological ideal of *ad orientem*. Navigational instruments were helping to provide a different notion of direction to liturgical practice. The development and use of north-pointing compasses in Europe and the Mediterranean from the thirteenth century meant that the negative religious associations of north began to shift, and were even replaced by a new sense of directionality, as another way of describing east in contrast to west started to appear. In his *Treatise on the Astrolabe* (written in the 1390s) the poet Geoffrey Chaucer described the use of the astronomical instrument to measure altitude and local latitudes with reference to the four cardinal directions, which he called 'principales plages' (derived from the Latin 'parts'). He outlined the form and construction of the main circular plate of the astrolabe as bisected by 'the est lyne or ellis the lyne oriental' and 'the west lyne or ellis the lyne occidentale'.[17] As a teaching manual Chaucer's book made no mention of theology or the importance of *ad orientem*. Instead it became part of the language of 'Orient', or 'rising', and its opposite, 'Occident', from the Latin for 'going down' or 'setting' (as in the Sun) that began to supplement the distinction between east and west.[18]

The demands of maritime trade and navigation in the Mediterranean using magnetic compasses were indifferent to sacred directions: for medieval Christian pilots, sailing safely from one port to another was more important than the direction of prayer, however pious they were. The 'East' as the place of Creation and just one of the four cardinal directions in seaborne navigation could coexist quite easily, depending on whether you were worshipping in church or sailing on business. Nobody knew this better than the Venetian merchant Marco Polo (c. 1254–1324). Between 1271 and 1295 he travelled along the Silk Road and seaborne trade routes that connected Europe and Asia, described in his book *The Travels of Marco Polo* (also known as the *Book of the Marvels of the World*), which began to circulate in various manuscript copies around 1300. Polo's account described 'the great wonders and curiosities of Greater Armenia and Persia, of the Tartars and of India', the Mongolian empire of Kublai Khan and China, called 'Cathay' or 'Manzi,' a derogatory Chinese word used by Mongols meaning 'barbarians of the south'.[19] Polo's east was oriented according to commercial centres like 'Kinsai' (modern-day Hangzhou) – what he called the 'City of Heaven' – and 'Khan-balik' (modern-day Beijing), rather than the biblical holy sites of Eden and Jersalem.[20]

The devotional connotations of the east, now increasingly referred to in another subtle shift by its Latin synonym 'Orient', were taking on increasingly mercantile associations in Europe towards the end of the fifteenth century. This was the consequence not only of Marco Polo's commercial land route into China, but also of long-distance seaborne navigation, especially the Iberian voyages into the Atlantic, the most famous of which were those of the Italian navigator Christopher Columbus. When

Columbus departed from Palos de la Frontera in south-western Spain in August 1492 he used magnetic compasses to sail west-wards with the intent of reaching the markets of Asia by sea, circumventing the established but long and expensive overland route. Even as he measured the direction of the North Pole in navigating 'west' to get to the 'east', magnetic variation meant that he had to compensate for declination registered by his compasses by sailing south.

Columbus's world picture remained suffused with medieval theological assumptions about cardinal directions. Having landed in the Bahamas in October 1492 – the first European to set foot on what came to be called the Americas since the Vikings 500 years earlier – Columbus was convinced he had reached Asia, even though the landscape and people he encountered seemed to bear little resemblance to medieval accounts of China, Japan or India. But he also imagined he had somehow travelled back in time into a world that brought him closer to the Earthly paradise in the east, or what he called the Orient. Sailing home in February 1493, Columbus wrote in his diary:

> The sacred theologians and learned philosophers were exactly correct when they said that the Earthly paradise is at the end of the Orient because it is a most temperate place. Those lands I have now discovered are . . . at the end of the Orient.[21]

Faith and geography collided, as Columbus acknowledged: 'Not that I believe the summit of the extreme point is navigable . . . or that it is possible to ascend to it.'[22] The eastern paradise was simultaneously of the Earth and beyond it.

East Meets West

With new maritime exploration in all four directions the Christian belief in the east as the direction of Paradise slowly waned and *mappae-mundi* no longer dominated the Christian world picture. The east shift changed from a sacred direction into a commercial destination with the growth of long-distance European voyages in the early sixteenth century. In 1494 the Treaty of Tordesillas agreed, in the wake of Columbus's voyages, to carve up the known world between the competing imperial powers of Spain and Portugal, drawing a line down the Atlantic 'three hundred and seventy leagues west of the Cape Verde Islands'. Everything on 'the western side of the said bound' belonged to Spain, while everything 'toward the east' belonged to Portugal.[23] Gradually, Paradise and the monstrous races faded from the margins of European world maps, and the east took on yet another layer of associations, a consequence of the pursuit of the riches of Asia spurred by the imperial competition between Spain and Portugal.

The voyages undertaken by the Italian navigator Amerigo Vespucci (1451–1512) between 1497 and 1504 named and proved beyond doubt that 'America' was a 'new world' to the west of Europe, a separate continent that was not part of Asia or the 'Indies' as Columbus believed. The first European circumnavigation of the globe between 1519 and 1522, led by the Portuguese explorer Ferdinand Magellan (1480–1521) and completed after his death, meant that sailing west from Europe to get to the east brought a clearer understanding of the global dimensions of the Earth.

One consequence of Magellan's voyage was the creation of distinct western and eastern hemispheres in the European geographical imagination. In the late 1520s Spain and Portugal debated where the meridian between their spheres of interest would fall in the disputed spice-producing islands of the Moluccas in the Indonesian archipelago, reached by the remains of Magellan's fleet in 1521. The result was a series of maps and globes that for the first time began to imagine eastern and western hemispheres, based primarily on the diplomatic dispute between the two imperial powers, with Portugal given dominion over the eastern hemisphere (Africa and Southeast Asia), Spain the west (primarily the Americas) – not that other empires like China or the Ottomans paid much attention to, or even knew about, such a fantastical division of the globe.

Nevertheless, as imperial conflict increased east and west between first Portugal and Spain and then England and Holland, the confusing language of the two directions remained. The 'Indies' (a term derived from India, the Sanskrit *sindhu*, meaning river, specifically the Indus) retained their power for Europeans as they travelled west, transplanting the term into North America and the Caribbean, mainly thanks to Columbus's conviction he had reached the 'Orient' in 1492. It was from here that the European imperial and colonial terms 'American Indians' and 'West Indies' come from, and they are still used, if somewhat contentiously, today (for instance the 'West Indies' cricket team).

*

In 1600 a group of English businessmen met to form the 'Company of Merchants trading into the East Indies' and to identify 'the principal places in the East Indies where trade is to be had'.[24] The East India Company, as it became known, would play a key role in English imperial ambitions in South Asia up to its demise by an Act of Parliament in 1874. But, like the Spanish, Portuguese and Dutch, the English East India Company pilots knew there was a practical navigational problem in establishing a safe and secure route to the east from Europe. Once again it involved time. Plotting a seaborne course east to west could not draw on any fixed astronomical points or magnetic poles, as was the case with north–south navigation, which could be calculated with some accuracy using degrees of latitude running north and south parallel to the Equator (notwithstanding the challenges of magnetic variation). Measuring distances on an east–west axis required map-makers and navigators to draw imaginary lines of longitude – also called meridians – running north–south from pole to pole either side of a prime meridian, which was only agreed on as Greenwich at the International Meridian Conference in Washington, DC, in 1884.

The problem in calculating longitude accurately was not just the lack of stars or poles: measuring distance east to west had to take into account the (prograde) rotation of the Earth. The answer was to measure time. Map-makers understood that local time in two places will vary with longitude, and that in any twenty-four hours the Earth rotates through 360 degrees. They also knew that one hour of time difference is equivalent to 15 degrees of longitude. If an absolute measure of time could be compared with any given local time, longitude could be accurately determined in minutes, seconds and degrees. The problem was creating an accurate timepiece that could measure time from its point of departure with another reference point while withstanding changing temperature, pressure, humidity and oceanic swells on-board ship. It was only with the invention of the marine chronometer using suspended mechanisms in the 1730s by the English clockmaker John Harrison (1693–1776) that accurate timekeeping at sea was ensured and with it the accurate measurement of longitude.

The effect of Harrison's solution to the longitude problem was to give the Royal Navy and English merchants a significant advantage in the eastern trade via the Cape of Good Hope. A new geopolitical outlook began to emerge in which the use of the compass and chronometer established 'west' and 'north' as co-extensive with Europe and a cluster of associations: civilized, inventive, prosperous. These were in opposition to values ascribed to the east (and by extension the south) and its inhabitants: barbaric, exotic and impoverished. The notion of the east first as a direction, then a place, was now being transformed by European travellers and merchants into an identity, encountering and defining whole peoples and cultures. As a result, 'the East' became a byword in the European imagination for certain attributes, beliefs and attitudes, from eastern philosophy and mysticism to religion, food and languages.

The Rise of Orientalism

The term 'orientalism' was first coined by the English historian Joseph Spence in 1747 when describing what he saw as the romantic, sublime 'higher Orientalism' of sections of Homer's *Odyssey*. For Spence, writing about the Old Testament, ancient Greek and Hebrew texts evoked a grandeur and exoticism associated with cultures and languages to the east of Europe. By the late eighteenth century the term took on greater precision as European travellers, merchants and scholars began a more systematic study of the language and literature of what came to be called the 'East'. Initially regarded as Turkey, Palestine, Syria and Arabia, it soon also included India, Japan and China. With such study came a belief in the innate superiority of European culture and negative assumptions about the qualities associated with 'eastern' nations and their people.

This orientalism gradually became more politicized throughout the nineteenth century, especially in the English-speaking world and with the rise of the British Empire in India. One particularly significant turning point came in 1835 when the British historian and Whig politician Thomas Babington Macaulay published his 'Minute on Indian Education' while sitting on the government's Supreme Council of India. Even though he had never set foot in India, Macaulay rejected its prevailing colonial educational system, which taught in Sanskrit and Arabic. Admitting blithely that he had 'no knowledge of Sanscrit [sic.] or Arabic', Macaulay maintained that, in talking to European orientalist scholars, 'I have never found one among them who could deny that a single shelf of a good European library was worth the whole native literature of India and Arabia.' Macaulay concluded, in a new colonial curriculum delivered to 'the learned natives of India', that 'we ought to employ them in teaching what is best worth knowing, that English is better worth knowing than Sanscrit or Arabic, that the natives are desirous to be taught English, and are not desirous to be taught Sanscrit or Arabic'.[25]

Just twelve years later the British Prime Minister Benjamin Disraeli would observe that the 'East is a career' in his novel *Tancred* (1847). Disraeli was pointing to the tradition of working in the British imperial administration in the 'Orient' established by imperial ideologues like Macaulay. Macaulay's combination of colonial presumption and historical ignorance was not limited to preoccupations about how the British should wield their authority in India. It was based on a much longer geopolitical myth of the East that stretched all the way back to Herodotus (c. 484–c. 425 BCE), admired by Macaulay as 'the earliest and best' classical historian. Such myths characterized the opening chapters of Herodotus's *Histories* (430 BCE). He divided the known world into three distinct continents: Europe, Asia and Africa (which he called Libya). But he also set up an enduring model of cultural difference and conflict between the opposing forces of east and west in his description of the wars between the Greek city-states and the Persian Empire in the fifth century BCE. In creating an absolute distinction between freedom-loving Athens and the despotic slavery of Persia, Herodotus traced their conflict all the way back to the Trojan Wars, claiming that, ever since, 'the Persians have always considered the Greeks to be their enemies. You see, the Persians regard Asia and the barbarian people who live in it as their domain, while they think of Europe and the Greeks as separate.'[26] Herodotus' binary opposition between the civilized West and the barbaric East was the beginning of a neoclassical move to designate ancient Greece as western when, as Spence argues, it could be seen as eastern or 'oriental'.

The reorientation of east and west was taken to its logical conclusion by the German philosopher Georg Wilhelm Friedrich Hegel (1770–1831) in his *Lectures on the Philosophy of History* (post. 1837), written in the same decade in which Macaulay was forming his views on 'oriental education' in India. Previous 'oriental' cultures such as the Chinese, Indian, Egyptian and Persian all represented inferior manifestations of the spirit of a nineteenth-century imperial Christian philosophy of history. They were categorized by despotism, irrationality, cruelty and barbarism. Nevertheless, for Hegel, 'The dawn of spirit is in the east, in the place of the Sun's rising.'[27] 'The History of the World,' wrote Hegel, 'travels from East to West, for Europe is absolutely the end of History, Asia the beginning.' In describing the philosophical development of the individual in world history, he went on, 'the first phase – that with which we have to begin – is the East', but it is 'the childhood of History. Substantial forms constitute the gorgeous edifices of Oriental Empires in which we find all rational ordinances and arrangements, but in such a way that individuals remain as mere accidents.' According to Hegel, it would take the development of enlightened European thought to develop these 'childish' early historical developments in the East, to truly realize the free 'world spirit'.[28]

Hegel's East was an outlandish myth steeped in notions of European intellectual superiority, the exclusive achievement of elite white men. It infantilized whole swathes of the Earth and its people, and justified the colonization and enslavement of much of Africa, Asia and the Americas. Hegel's own views on race and slavery included the belief that Columbus was a hero dragging indigenous people into an awareness of their real 'spirit' and that slavery should only be phased out gradually as black Africans came to truly 'know' themselves.[29] Despite all this, the geopolitical and philosophical outlines of Hegel's world history still hold sway among many in the 'western' world, who regard 'eastern' culture as lacking in 'civilized' values.

The beliefs, actions and consequences of thinkers and politicians including Macaulay and Hegel were only seriously challenged in the later twentieth century, following the postwar period of decolonization, by writers such as the Palestinian critic Edward Said. His book *Orientalism* (1978) was the first sustained challenge to the European orientalist tradition. In it he accepted the established designation of orientalism as primarily a scholarly and academic endeavour, but he went much further. For him, Europe created an image of the East, or Orient, in the act of defining itself as the West: one could not exist without the other. Orientalism was almost exclusively one-sided, driven by Europe's projection of its own hopes and fears. 'The Orient,' wrote Said, 'is not only adjacent to Europe; it is also the place of Europe's greatest and richest and oldest colonies, the source of its civilizations and languages, its cultural contestant, and one of its deepest and most recurring images of the Other.' As a consequence, 'the Orient has helped to define Europe (or the West) as its contrasting image, idea, personality, experience. Yet none of this Orient is merely imaginative. The Orient is an integral part of European material civilization and culture.' Without a political projection of the 'East', there is no 'West'. In describing somewhere as 'elsewhere', European orientalists were of course describing 'here', their own culture, beliefs and *habitus*.

Said argued that orientalism was not just an academic and creative act, but also a deeply political and coercive process that created 'the corporate institution for dealing with the Orient – dealing with it by making statements about it, authorizing views of it, describing it, by teaching it, settling it, ruling over it: in short, Orientalism as a Western style for dominating, restructuring, and having authority over the Orient'. For Said, the Orient was an invention of European thinkers, artists and politicians, practising what Said called 'imaginative geography'. Nowhere was this practice more evocative than in its creation of the concept of 'the Middle East', a term first coined by the British India Office in 1850. But its modern geopolitical and strategic meaning was developed by the American naval strategist Alfred Mahan in 1902 to help describe British and Russian imperial claims to an area he described as stretching between 'Arabia and India'. Yet, like so many geopolitical definitions drawn from the four cardinal directions, over time and for different people the 'Middle East' became a politically moving target, stretching from Cairo all the way to Burma, depending on shifting and competing European colonial claims to the region.

Today, Western organizations like the US State Department refer matters relating to what is named the 'Middle East' to its Bureau of Near Eastern Affairs (NEA), also known rather confusingly as the Bureau of Near East Asian Affairs, which is broken down into ten sub-regional offices, including ones for Levant, Maghreb and Arabian Peninsula affairs. According to the NEA, Mauritania, Cyprus and Afghanistan are not in the Near East, but Morocco and Pakistan are. The UN Food and Agriculture Organization disagrees, while the Washington Institute for Near East Policy (WINEP) tries – but doesn't always succeed – to stay in line with the US State Department's nomenclature. It is no wonder that US policy in the region is accused of being biased and ineffectual when it seems incapable of any consistency in even naming the area.

The East and its division into 'Near', 'Middle' and 'Far' has a long history in the Western imperial imagination. One of its most celebrated poetic descriptions was inspired by the North-West Frontier of Pakistan and Afghanistan under British imperial rule. It came from that enthusiastic supporter of the British Empire Rudyard Kipling, and his poem 'The Ballad of East and West' (1889). Kipling opens with the famous claim about the absolute difference between Orient and Occident:

> Oh, East is East, and West is West, and never the twain
>   shall meet

This line and much of the poem's sentiment is inspired by a verse from Psalm 103: 'As far as the east is from the west, so far has He removed our transgressions from us' (Psalms 103:12). God's ability to forgive sin is seen here as infinite, and like east and west, once removed, sin can never return: similarly, without a fixed point or 'pole', east and west can never meet: if one travels westwards, it is never possible to reach a point and begin going eastwards, or vice versa. As far as a compass is concerned, we can travel eastwards for ever. This is in contrast to travelling north or south, where eventually you will meet one of the poles, and begin moving in the 'opposite' direction. Or, at least, that's what the power of the imaginative geography of the poles will make you believe. But Kipling goes on immediately to qualify this initially absolute division of cardinal directions:

> Till Earth and Sky stand presently at God's great
>   Judgment Seat;

But there is neither East nor West, Border,
    nor Breed, nor Birth,
When two strong men stand face to face, though they come
    from the ends of the Earth!

The boundaries between East and West will dissolve on the Christian Judgement Day, or when two warriors from the two cultures test each other's masculinity, which is precisely what Kipling describes in the poem's encounter between an Afghan raider and a British soldier. After clashing, they come to a mutual admiration of each other, taking 'the Oath of Brother-in-Blood'. The poem ends by repeating its first stanza, reiterating the limitations of social divisions between East and West. But such an idealized image depends entirely on Kipling's Western, imperial and Christian masculinity: everything is on the Western writer's terms, as he creates an idea of the East – and West – before dismissing them in the face of an English imperial myth of male friendship that transcends race and religion – and ignores women altogether.

Kipling's poem exemplifies Said's argument that the idea of the 'Orient' as a place inhabited by 'Oriental' people is purely a fictional creation of Western writing and thinking. And yet it has proved to be a powerful and prevailing story. In his short essay 'East Indian' written in 1965, V. S. Naipaul captures something of the black comedy of the confusions wrought by colonization around the terms 'east' and 'west' and those required to – quite literally – labour under them. Born in Trinidad of Indian heritage, Naipaul was particularly alert to the fact that to 'be an Indian or East Indian from the West Indies is to be a perpetual surprise to people outside the region . . . So long as the real Indians remained on the other side of the world, there was little confusion.' But once Indian indentured labour started being transported to the Caribbean in the 1840s, 'confusion became total'. Under British colonial dominion, 'the immigrants were called East Indians' to distinguish them from 'the American Indians and the West Indians. After a generation or two, the East Indians were regarded as settled inhabitants of the West Indies and were thought of as West Indian East Indians. Then a national feeling grew up. There was a cry for integration, and the West Indian East Indians became East Indian West Indians.'[30] 'East' both as a direction and an identity was ever mobile.

The View from the East

Not everyone described in Europe's orientalist fantasies of the East accepted these stereotypes. From the late eighteenth century, when the European imperial powers started to establish a presence in China, the Qing dynasty (1644–1911) began to reorient its place in the world. China had always regarded itself as *Zhongguo*, the 'Middle Kingdom', at the centre of the world. The emergence of the West in geopolitics prompted China to begin identifying itself self-consciously as 'eastern' from the late nineteenth century. This took on even greater significance under Mao Zedong's Cultural Revolution (1966–76): eager to position itself opposing the bourgeois capitalist West, Chinese Communist Party propaganda appropriated the visual iconography of the East and the rising Sun as a symbol of Mao's rule. The unofficial anthem of the Cultural Revolution was even entitled 'The East is Red', celebrating the dawn of a new era of proletarian revolution under Mao:

Here in the East rises a sun,
China has brought forth a Mao Zedong . . .
The Communist Party is like the sun . . .
It brings a great revolution!

It was part of a wider geopolitical alignment of East and West following the end of the Second World War in 1945. From China to Vietnam, Czechoslovakia and Poland, the East became synonymous with Marxist-Leninist Communism – East Timor, eastern Europe, East Germany, East Berlin. The East was no longer the location of exotic places to colonize, but a movable site of Communist states from Beijing to Warsaw, locked in an existential conflict with its binary opposite, the West. With the fall of the Berlin Wall in 1989 and the collapse of the Soviet Union in 1991, one moment of political geography between East and West came to an end – only then to re-form in the current global economy.

As a result, today China has a conflicted relationship between its sense of being East while also embracing the West. The Chinese state sees itself as in the ascendancy in the East, in contrast to what it regards as the economic and political decline of the West. For the political elite in Beijing, the globalized world has shifted eastwards, centred on a Chinese state that demands the West acknowledge its pre-eminence. Yet, at a more popular level, the West remains the direction to be dreamt of and the destination to desire for many Chinese people. Despite propagandist attempts to counter the myth of the 'American Dream' with the 'China Dream' concocted since 2012, the Chinese are still leaving their country and moving from east to west in record numbers.[31]

*

The idea of the East has travelled a long way, politically and geographically, through space and across time, since its earliest associations with the Sun rising. From animistic and polytheistic Sun worship, to Abrahamic beliefs in the eastern origins of Creation, it has become a mobile marker of cultural origins and personal identity. It has also lost its purely directional meaning more profoundly than any other direction: the development of artificially lit, high-rise urban environments mean that many of us city dwellers rarely if ever see the horizon, or the Sun rising, because of the rhythm of modern working life. We have become quite literally 'disoriented'.

Today, what is understood as the East is changing its geopolitical meaning more rapidly than any other cardinal direction, wherever you live on the globe. China lies behind much of this reorientation. In 2013 the Chinese leader Xi Jinping announced the 'Belt and Road' initiative (BRI) – also known as 'One Belt One Road' and the 'Silk Road Economic Belt'. As this last description suggests, it represents a new 'Silk Road', running from east to west, yet its scale is on an altogether different level. The initiative involves Chinese political and economic investment in infrastructure development in 155 countries, affecting nearly 75 per cent of the world's population and half of its GDP, stretching across sea and land from Beijing to Venice. Supporters see the BRI as driving unparalleled global economic growth and uniting Asia, Africa and Europe as never before; critics see it as a sign of China buying international political influence and monopolizing global trade networks, regardless of concerns over the environment and human rights. Whatever its outcome, BRI is redefining global conceptions of the East and returning itself from Mao's 'eastern' Communist power to the older imperial idea of *Zhongguo*: China as the 'Middle Kingdom' sitting at the centre of the world.[32]

Traditional European colonial presumptions about the East are also heading in a different direction. Much of what has been called the 'East' is now part of the 'Global South', developing a political axis that challenges the pre-eminence of the overlapping polities of the developed North and West. The East is no longer the site for a European colonial career, nor even simply the emblem of daily renewal and the passage of time, but the

location of some of the globe's most dynamic economies –
Singapore, South Korea, Vietnam, Taiwan – and what may soon
be the world's largest economy of all: China. It is the direction
of the global future.

SOUTH

Southern Comfort

'Every culture has its southerners,' wrote Susan Sontag in her novel *The Volcano Lover* (1992). Following her account of Palermo, the capital of Sicily, 'the south of the south', she describes southerners as

> people who work as little as they can, preferring to dance, drink, sing, brawl, kill their unfaithful spouses; who have livelier gestures, more lustrous eyes, more colourful garments, more fancifully decorated vehicles, a wonderful sense of rhythm, and charm, charm, charm; unambitious, no, lazy, ignorant, superstitious, uninhibited people, never on time, conspicuously poorer (how could it be otherwise, say the northerners); who for all their poverty and squalor lead enviable lives – envied, that is, by work-driven, sensually inhibited, less corruptly governed northerners. We are superior to them, say the northerners, clearly superior. We do not shirk our duties or tell lies as a matter of course, we work hard, we are punctual, we keep reliable accounts. But they have more fun than we do.

For northerners and their work ethic, southerners are seductive because 'if you start dancing on tables, fanning yourself, feeling sleepy when you pick up a book, developing a sense of rhythm, making love whenever you feel like it – then you know. The south has got you.'[1]

Sontag's celebration of the south is a knowing literary cliché from a Northern European perspective. The Sardinian Marxist philosopher Antonio Gramsci (1891–1937) understood this only too well in his essay 'The Southern Question' (1926). Gramsci believed that the stereotypes of the south were a political and ideological myth designed to mask deeper economic conflicts in Italy: 'the South is the ball and chain which prevents the social development of Italy from progressing more rapidly; the Southerners are biologically inferior beings, semi-barbarians or total barbarians, by natural destiny; if the South is backward, the fault does not lie with the capitalist system or with any other historical cause, but with Nature, which has made the Southerners lazy, incapable, criminal and barbaric.'[2]

In their different ways both Sontag and Gramsci acknowledged that south is not only a geographical space and personal identity: it is an idea. In contrast to the east–west axis, both versions of the south, the seductive and the backward, were defined by contrast with the north. The south has for centuries appeared bereft of history, a repository for the northern hemisphere's ideas and fantasies, and the only cardinal direction that has depth as a measure of its extent – as in the 'deep south' and 'down south'.

This sense of the south as a fluid, intangible idea has provided rich material for writers. In Jorge Luis Borges's short story 'The South' ('El Sur' in the original Spanish), written in 1953, the central character, Juan Dahlmann, leaves Buenos Aires to convalesce on 'a ranch in the South'. According to Borges, 'Every Argentine knows that the South begins at the other side of Rivadavia', in the vast plains or *Pampas* in the south-east of the country. Taking the train, Dahlmann is dimly aware he 'was travelling into the past and not merely the south'. Challenged to a fight at a local store, he is thrown a knife by a gaucho, 'a summary and cipher of the South . . . it was if the South had resolved that Dahlmann should accept the duel'. Sensing his doom, Dahlmann is suddenly convinced this is the death he would have chosen, and walks 'out into the plain' of the south to an uncertain fate.

Read at various times as an allegory of Argentina's mixed European–American colonial heritage and a reflection on illusion versus reality, at the heart of Borges's story are notions of the south as the site of an authentic, indigenous Argentina, as an unreachable place, and as a shifting state of mind. Admirers of Borges such as Salman Rushdie also grasped the south as a mirage. Rushdie's 'In the South' (2009) reflects on mortality from the perspective of two friends, known only as Junior and Senior. When Junior describes himself in Sontag's terms as a 'warm, slow, and sensual' southerner in contrast to 'the cold fishes of the north', Senior retorts:

the south is a fiction, existing only because men have agreed to call it that. Suppose men had imagined the Earth the other way up! We would be the northerners then. The universe does not understand up and down; neither does a dog. To a dog, there is no north or south. In this regard, the points of the compass are like money, which has value only because men say that it does.[3]

The Beautiful South

The power of the south can be traced back at least as far as ancient Egypt. The rising Sun to the east brought life and was personified as the solar deity and original creator, Ra, but the north–south axis also powerfully influenced the rhythms of everyday life. These were almost exclusively marked by the fertile Nile river which flows from its origins in Upper Egypt in the south – and its origins beyond that in East Africa – to Lower Egypt to the north, where it discharges into the Mediterranean. South became the prime direction. The terms *hynty* ('in front' or 'south of') and *phwy* ('behind' or 'north of'), along with the Egyptian words for east (*isbt*) and west (*imnt*) – 'left' and 'right' respectively – all corroborate an orientation in which south took precedence, also reflected by the usual order in enumeration of south, north, west, east in ancient Egyptian culture.[4]

But even here any clear-cut understanding of sacred directional axes was complicated by the physical geography of Egypt. In the archaic period (*c.* 3150–*c.* 2686 BCE) the singular northward flow of the Nile through Upper Egypt meant that north and south were immediately recognizable and imagined as the prime directional axis. But in Lower Egypt, where the Nile splits into various tributaries and creates the vast life-giving delta from Alexandria to Port Said, it proved harder to envisage a simple north–south orientation rather than to trace the clearer east–west movement of the Sun.

These Egyptian orientations were given visual form in various funerary pictograms, represented on the cover of a surviving stone sarcophagus (Plate 11) dated to the Thirtieth Dynasty (*c.* 350 BCE). In this elegant cosmology the symmetries of the two cardinal axes are unified in the dominating figure of the sky goddess Nut, whose curved body forms the dome of the heavens (including the stars and the Sun's movement shown at the top) as she bends over, her hands on the same plane as her feet. Between them is the Earth-god Geb supporting the circular world; above it sits Shu, god of light and air and supporter of the sky. The outer ring depicts various neighbouring communities beyond Egypt's borders, with the limbs of the goddesses of the east on the left and of the west on the right curving around the circle, their raised arms supporting two Sun boats sailing across the firmament. This orients the pictogram with south and Upper Egypt at the top. The innermost circle depicts Egypt divided into its various *nomes*, or regional districts.

The sarcophagus's terrestrial world oriented with south at the top could still accommodate the cosmology of death and rebirth imagined as following the east–west axis of sunrise and sunset. This cosmography finds its apex in the sacred architectural orientation of the greatest of all funerary monuments: the ancient pyramids. Built on the western bank of the Nile and formed of a square base oriented according to the four cardinal directions, the apex of each pyramid pointed towards the polar star, regarded as the gateway to the heavens and afterlife. Through a series of elaborate funerary rites preparing the dead body with its paraphernalia, the pharaoh would be made ready to ascend the sky northwards then follow the westwards movement of the setting Sun towards the home of the dead in anticipation of rebirth and immortality.[5]

Early Islamic thinking also oriented its cosmology to the south, but for very different reasons and without any apparent influence from the ancient Egyptian tradition. Islamic cosmology drew extensively though unevenly on Judaic, Greek, Christian and even the Zoroastrian beliefs practised in ancient Iran.[6] While living in Medina, Muhammad's *qibla*, the sacred direction of prayer, lay due south, the direction of Mecca. Zoroastrian belief also privileged south as the prime direction, and this, combined with early Islamic belief during Muhammad's life in Medina, led some Arabic dialects in Egypt and Palestine to use the word *qibla* as a synonym for 'south'. As many of the tribes due north of Medina converted to Islam, *qibla* was initially due south, leading most (though not all) Islamic world maps to position south at the top.

By the tenth century, Islamic map-making in the Abbasid caliphate centred on Baghdad produced various maps, from theoretical cosmologies to more practical ones. One particularly influential dimension was that known as *Kitab al-masalik wa-al-mamalik* ('Books of routes and realms'), concerned with trade, pilgrimage and administration. This tradition is exemplified by a relatively unknown map-maker, Muhammad al-Istakhri, active in the late tenth century. A Persian copy of al-Istakhri's world map, dated 1297, shows the land mass in the central circle oriented with south at the top (Plate 12). Africa is a large claw extending deep into the Indian Ocean at top left, and the vertical bar running from top right downwards is the Nile, flowing into th e Mediterranean with three red circular islands: Cyprus, Crete and Sicily. The triangle below these three represents Europe, with Muslim Spain (*al-Andalus*) labelled at its apex. The map's finest detail lies at the heart of the Muslim Empire, whose various administrative districts are neatly demarcated in red. Arabia sits at the heart of the map with the prominent holy sites of Mecca and Medina.[7]

As we have seen, Christian *mappae-mundi* from the same period were oriented with east as their cardinal direction on religious grounds. Most Muslim maps, following al-Istakhri, chose south for similar reasons, but with very different visual and religious outcomes. As the Islamic Empire grew and spread into North Africa and Asia over subsequent centuries, calculating the *qibla* to ensure the correct directions of prayer towards Mecca became increasingly complex. Maps such as al-Istakhri's show that, although the southern sacred orientation placed Mecca at its centre, nearly half the terrestrial globe still stretched 'up' into the unknown southern lands of sub-Saharan Africa, way beyond yet another hazily projected idea about the origins of the Nile. The south stretched upwards and onwards, with no end in sight.

On the other side of the globe in medieval Iceland, the south was also adopted as the cardinal direction, but because of yet another perspective. Medieval Icelandic scholars absorbed classical and early Christian traditions of mapping the world according to the three continents of Asia, Europe and Africa, but turned the prevailing eastern orientation 90 degrees anti-clockwise to place south at the top of their maps. On a hemispherical world map dated to around 1300–1325, the anonymous Icelandic map-maker combined Latin and Old Norse transcriptions to create a map oriented southwards, and at its centre a schematic map showing *Asia* to the left, *Affrica* to the right, and *Europa* below (Plate 13). The map shows the Earth divided into climates, with polar circles, the two tropics and the Equator. The orbits of the Sun and the Moon are shown along with the signs of the zodiac, and around the whole world (described in Old Norse as *um alla uerold*) is the ocean (*Megin haf*). In the middle of the map is the phrase *Synnri bygo*, Old Norse for 'southern inhabitable land'. Drawing on a combination of classical, Christian and Icelandic beliefs, it places south at the top because of Icelanders' sense of their location at the northernmost periphery of Europe. Lying just south of the Arctic Circle between 63.4°N and 66.5°N and inhabiting one of the most northerly latitudes within Europe, Icelanders then and now look 'down' south towards the inhabited world, with the dark, inhospitable north 'behind' them.[8]

Classical Chinese cosmology also celebrated the south, but this was based on more political and imperial expectations. In Chinese 'south' (*nan*) was expressed in its archaic pictograph as a liana plant, evoking the luxuriant vegetation of the south as viewed from the drier, colder northern latitudes. South was the direction of fertility, warmth and abundance. It also gave rise to what were known as south-pointing chariots (or carriages), two-wheeled vehicles with a geared mechanism and containing a figure point-ing south. The origins, mechanics and function of these chariots remain the subject of dispute, though they appear to have been used from the first millennium BCE to conduct envoys back home once they re-entered Chinese territories. These ceremonial dimensions also affected imperial power. During important events and audiences, emperors sat in the 'dragon's chair', which looked south, with the phrase 'facing south' a proper noun synonymous with 'emperor', and 'to face south' meaning to become an emperor, who looked 'down', southwards, to his subjects, who looked 'up', or northwards, in deference to their ruler. This imperial cardinal hierarchy was repeated in courts, schools and even homes where the south-facing seat was reserved for the highest-ranking official, teacher or member of the household.[9] For this reason the orientation of most early Chinese maps placed north at the top, with the imperial subjects gazing up northwards towards the emperor who looked south in the direction of growth and plenitude.

Central to the Confucian principle of *qiang*, which can mean 'energy', 'tenacity' or 'force', was an understanding of balance. In the early Confucian classic *Zongyong* ('The Doctrine of the Mean'), when the impulsive disciple Zilu questions Confucius about energy, he responds by describing a balance between north and south:

> Zilu asked about energy. The Master said, 'Do you mean the energy of the South, the energy of the North, or the energy which you should cultivate yourself? To show forbearance and gentleness in teaching others, and not to revenge unreasonable conduct: this is the energy of Southern regions, and the good man makes it his study. To lie under arms, and meet death without regret: this is the energy of Northern regions, and the forceful make it their study. Therefore, the superior man cultivates a friendly harmony, without being weak. How firm is he in his energy! He stands erect in the middle, without inclining to either side.'[10]

A temperate balance between southern reflective and northern warlike energy enabled the cultivation of a mean point between the two forces.

Newfound South

Greek ideas on the cardinal directions from Aristotle to Timosthenes bequeathed two concepts adapted by Christianity. The first was Aristotle's belief that the Earth was divided into five climates: they included the two polar zones – the northern Artic, or *Arktos*, named after the northern constellation of the Great Bear, and its opposite, Antarctic – and a temperate, southern continent: the Antipodes. This became the basis of the modern understanding of Australia and New Zealand as the Antipodes; indeed, 'Australia' comes from the Latin *auster*, or south, used to describe the wind. Thousands of years before Europeans reached this southerly region named as *terra Australis*, Aristotle had already anticipated its existence. The second idea was the ethnological dimension of direction. Timosthenes labelled three southern winds (*Notus*) as synonymous with Ethiopia, a catch-all Greco-Roman term for Africa.

In the European Middle Ages, the Greco-Roman tradition was modified to fit a biblical vision of Creation. 'The South', according to Isidore of Seville (*c.* 560–636 CE) in his hugely influential *Etymologies*, is *meridies*, 'and is so named either because there the Sun makes midday (*medium diem*) as if the world were *medidie*, or because at that time the aether sparkles more purely, for *merus* means pure. The sky has two portals: the east and the west, for the Sun enters through one portal and withdraws through the other.'[11] Medieval *mappae-mundi* depicted the south ranging from Ethiopia and the Nile in Africa, to India and Taprobana (Sri Lanka) in Asia, with anything further south than that labelled *terra incognita*: the south was simply 'unknown land'. The 'purity' that Isidore identified from the word's classical etymology quickly waned, and various negative associations began to develop in relation to south. The direction was regarded as

being populated by uncivilized, nomadic, warlike (yet also simultaneously indolent) people and fantastic creatures, snakes being
a particular favourite.

As the monstrous animals and races faded from medieval
maps, Renaissance map-makers fused navigational science with
prevailing stereotypes about the south to produce racialized
wind-heads (a decorative feature depicting personifications of
the winds) that often showed the southern directions as clichéd
black figures with curly hair (Plate 15). For northern Europeans,
the south was no longer the direction of monstrosity but still
an amorphous place of exotic yet fearful racial difference.[12] The
European literary imagination, fuelled by the belief in a vast,
temperate southern continent, projected various fears but also
aspirations on to this as yet undiscovered 'no-place' – or 'Utopia'.
Two of the most influential Renaissance texts, Thomas More's
Utopia (1516) and Francis Bacon's *New Atlantis* (1626), first set
their ideal worlds in the south: More in the Indian Ocean south
of Calicut, and Bacon west of Peru in the Pacific, or what he calls
'the South Sea'. From there, the worlds they envisage take on a
very different meaning, driven by a perception of the south as a
place of endless possibility and renewal.

The practical reality of European seaborne travel to and discovery of a projected 'terra Australis' proved more frustrating,
fuelled by an ever-shifting perception of the idea and location of
the south. In the 1640s the Dutch reached the west coast of Australia – first named 'New Holland' – and Tasmania – after Abel
Janszoon Tasman – but were unclear if this was indeed a new
southern continent or just another island. By the early seventeenth century long-distance seaborne travel was focused on
east–west voyages connecting the Americas with Asia, in contrast to voyaging north–south over the poles, which was believed
would result only in death amidst extreme climates of heat or ice.

But the lure of the south remained. In 1711 the British government backed the creation of the South Sea Company, a joint-stock organization aimed at reducing the national debt by trading in African slaves in the Americas and the 'South Seas'. But, with the Spanish and Portuguese effectively monopolizing the slave trade, the company collapsed in 1720, leaving its investors ruined in what became known as the 'South Sea Bubble'. One of the most serious political and economic crises in Georgian England was partly caused by the purely imaginative projection of a barely known 'south' on the other side of the world.

Undaunted by such economic folly, the British Admiralty and the Royal Society continued to invest in the exploration of the 'South Seas'. In 1767 Alexander Dalrymple, a Scottish explorer, fellow of the Royal Society and hydrographer to the Admiralty, published *An Account of the Discoveries Made in the South Pacifick Ocean*. In it he announced that a 'continent is wanting on the south of the Equator, to counterpoise the land on the north, and to maintain the equilibrium necessary for the Earth's motion'.[13] Such claims fuelled the decision by the Admiralty and Royal Society to finance a voyage to the Pacific to observe the transit of Venus (to estimate the Earth's distance from the Sun) and search for and claim the elusive southern continent. Captain James Cook (1728–79) was chosen to lead the expedition.

In his three voyages to the Pacific between 1768 and 1779, Cook explored further south – an estimated 71°10' S – than any previously known human. He also travelled further northwards than anyone else in recorded history to that time, reaching a latitude of 70°44' north along the Alaskan coast in August 1778. Having set off on his first voyage, Cook opened the Admiralty's secret orders that told him to search for the ultimate southern destination: 'Terra Australis'. On 31 March 1770, towards the end of his first voyage on HMS *Endeavour* to Tahiti, Australia and New Zealand, he claimed to have disproved 'most, if not all, the arguments and proofs that have been advanced by different authors to prove that there must be a Southern Continent'.[14] He was convinced that 'no man will ever venture farther than I have done and that the lands which may lie to the South will never be explored'. Cook had travelled south through and beyond Aristotle's imagined temperate zone, minus its projected great continent, and onwards to its southern antithesis: on 17 January 1773 Cook crossed into the freezing Antarctic Circle before turning back. Yet again the southernmost point on the globe still seemed just out of reach, though Cook, for very good reasons, thought it was a region of

> lands doomed by nature to everlasting frigidness and never once to feel the warmth of the sun's rays, whose horrible and savage aspect I have no words to describe; such are the lands we have discovered; what may we expect those to be which lie more to the South, for we may reasonably suppose that we have seen the best as lying most to the North, whoever has resolution and perseverance to clear up this point by proceeding farther than I have done, I shall not envy him the honour of the discovery but I will be bold to say that the world will not be benefited by it.

True south now lay even further away, this time encased in ice: Cook's voyages had ended one European myth of its terminus.

But just as Cook concluded a chapter on one fable of the south, he was responsible for revising another. In April 1769 HMS *Endeavour* landed in Tahiti in the South Pacific archipelago now known as the Society Islands. Cook was by no means the first European to reach Tahiti. A year earlier Louis Antoine, Comte de Bougainville, reached the island on his journey to become the first Frenchman to navigate the globe. What de Bougainville saw there was a new version of paradise, a prelapsarian world more familiar to Christian visions of the east, now relocated to the south. 'The sweetness of the climate,' he enthused, 'the beauty of the landscape, the fertility of the ground which is everywhere fed by streams and waterfalls', led him to name Tahiti 'La Nouvelle Cythère' – 'the new island of Love'.[15] The South Seas and its islands were a new Eden on to which Europeans could project their more enlightened and romantic fantasies of beginning anew and living at one with nature.

Cook, however, had a more prosaic view of the island. He disapproved of the sexual bartering between his sailors and the Tahitian women, which was partly responsible for the theft and violence that came to characterize relations between the Europeans and the Pacific islanders. As alcohol and diseases such as syphilis and tuberculosis decimated the islands thanks to the European pursuit of Eden, the region became a paradise lost. Yet the myth of the south continued to influence European writers and artists eager to embrace the south's wonder. When the German naturalist and explorer Alexander von Humboldt travelled to the Spanish Americas in 1799, he approached the Equator and the southern continent with a sense of awe. 'From the time we entered the torrid zone,' Humboldt wrote,

we were never wearied with admiring, every night, the beauty of the southern sky, which, as we advanced towards the south . . . this sight fills with admiration even those who, uninstructed in the branches of accurate science, feel the same emotion of delight in the contemplation of the heavenly vault, as in the view of a beautiful landscape or a majestic sight . . . everything in the equinoctial regions assumes an exotic character.[16]

Antifreeze

Cook's exploration of the inhospitable Antarctic region also gave rise to a perception of the south as no longer a paradise, but more of a sublime and terrifyingly empty frozen wilderness. As a result, a more darkly romantic, even gothic version of the south began to emerge in the nineteenth-century European imagination. Once again, notions of the region as the southernmost point of the Earth originated in its opposite direction, the Arctic north. Even its name – 'anti-Arctic' – indicated how much older perceptions determined connotations of the far north. But the extreme south that the first Europeans discovered when they landed on Antarctica in the 1820s turned out to be very different to its northern counterpart. Whereas the Arctic is an ocean covered by ice and surrounded by land, Antarctica is a continent surrounded by ocean, a continent made of ice 2,700 kilometres deep, in contrast to the Arctic's 2–3 metres. With winter temperatures sometimes reaching minus 136 degrees Fahrenheit, Antarctica is three times colder on average than the Arctic and towers up to 2,800 metres above sea level. But the most powerful difference is human habitation: whereas the Arctic has been populated continuously since 12,000 BCE, no human ever set foot on Antarctica before the 1820s, and even today it has no permanent human population.

The transformation of Antarctica from a shifting, temperate paradise to a colder and isolated place was captured most famously in Samuel Taylor Coleridge's 'The Rime of the Ancient Mariner'. Written in 1797 and first published the following year in *Lyrical Ballads*, a joint collection by Wordsworth and Coleridge, his poem is central to the development of the English Romantic movement. Its description of the mariner who seeks redemption after killing an albatross drew on Cook's voyages and his foray into the Antarctic Circle in 1773. The first stanzas of Coleridge's poem locate the mariner's description of a voyage in the frozen south, as his ship 'drove fast, loud roared the blast, / And southward aye we fled'. A storm 'chased us south' from the Equator and the fateful encounter with the albatross. For Coleridge, the frozen, empty south is as much a symbol of the mariner's subsequent descent into a desolate, existential hell and his pursuit of redemption as a physical location. The south was now a journey into the mind as well as a voyage to a place with fixed coordinates on a map.

Coleridge's poem was a chilling prefiguration of one of the most romantic yet ultimately tragic pursuits of the south: the race to the South Pole that led to the deaths of the English explorer Captain Robert Falcon Scott (1868–1912) and his companions. It is a testament to the power of Scott's doomed expedition and his rivalry with the Norwegian explorer Roald Amundsen that his story has been told countless times. Central to its attraction is one man's fatal confrontation with the elements and the great southern wilderness, the most inhospitable place on Earth.

Scott and his team were painfully aware of their legacy as explorers of the last blank space in the southern hemisphere. In his memoir of Scott's ill-fated expedition, *The Worst Journey in the World* (1922), Apsley Cherry-Garrard (1886–1959) – one of the expedition's few survivors – placed Scott in the pantheon of famous southern explorers: 'Cook, Ross and Scott: these are the aristocrats of the South.' Another member of Scott's previous failed journey to the pole, the celebrated Antarctic explorer Sir Ernest Shackleton, later claimed that he himself always 'felt strangely drawn towards the mysterious south', to 'go to the region of ice and snow and go on and on till I came to the poles of the Earth, the end of the axis upon which this great ball turns'.

This was an aspiration worthy of Aristotle's perception of the Earth in his *Meteorology*. But for Scott it brought nothing other than failure and a lonely death by exposure to the extreme cold.

By the time he reached the geographic South Pole on 17 January 1912, thirty-four days after Amundsen, Scott's dream had evaporated. Reaching the Pole had all been pointless, literally and metaphorically. Technically it is just a coordinate: there is nothing actually there to demarcate it from the wilderness of ice and snow. 'The Pole. Yes, but under very different circumstances from those we expected,' wrote Scott on the same day. 'Great God!' he famously concluded, 'this is an awful place.' On 29 or 30 March he died in what he had described as 'the eternal silence of the great white desert'.[17]

Scott's heroic – or needless – death, was a particularly resonant instance of a much larger range of gothic and fantastic projections of the south as an uninhabited, even alien world where the most outlandish ideas could be tested. Subsequent notions of the South Pole ranged from its point as an entry into a hollow Earth, the site of lost, ancient and otherworldly civilizations described in science-fiction novels, to the location of a secret Nazi base where Adolf Hitler escaped at the end of the Second World War. With the North Pole firmly established at the 'top' of the world, and the South Pole unquestionably at its 'bottom', Antarctica became a psychic underworld that according to the literary critic Elizabeth Leane mirrored the topography of the mind:

> At least since Freud, parallels between mental and physical landscapes have frequently assumed a depth model of the psyche, with the darker, less accessible aspects of ourselves – the Id, in Freud's terms – imagined us sitting somehow 'below the surface'. This means that the metaphorical southern journey is not simply a journey inwards but also downwards,

a journey that penetrates the darkest, deepest regions of the unconscious.[18]

The globe, like the human skull and the mind encased within, was a projection of our interior psychological world. Whereas the North Pole was the entrance into the mind, at its 'bottom' lay the South Pole, impenetrable and unknown, its forbidding environment utterly indifferent to human endeavour.

A World Turned Upside Down

As a repository for the release of so many primal and instinctive human impulses, the south also enabled those people labelled 'southerners' without their consent to speak back against their positioning by the north. By the end of the nineteenth century such voices came most eloquently not from Europe or the Antarctic, but the Americas. Anti-colonial struggles for independence swept the American continent during the lifetimes of both Coleridge and Scott. Those in modern-day South America – named thanks to a prevailing north–south conception of the world that originated in Europe – struggled to find a new 'southern' identity by opposing the colonial north. Increasingly, countries designated south and east across Africa, Asia and the Americas allied themselves ideologically in opposition to the imperial and economic powers in the north and west, represented by Europe and North America. Northern denigration of the south only intensified as their colonial domination was questioned and challenged, as expressed by contemporary popular American writers such as Charles Fort (1874–1932):

It is upon the northern parts of this Earth that the civilizations that have persisted have grown up, then extending themselves colonially southward. History, like South America and Africa, tapers southward. There are no ruins of temples, pyramids, obelisks in Australia, Argentina, South Africa . . . Life withers southward . . . If this Earth be top-shaped as some of the geodesists think, it is a bloom that is stemmed with desolation.[19]

Yet the rejection of such views had a long history too. The Cuban poet and revolutionary activist José Julián Martí Pérez (1853–95) spoke for much of South America's desire for independence in his book *Our America* (1891). Martí believed 'We must leave the North behind' if the region was to reclaim a collective identity free from Europe, yet also embrace its complex *mestiza* heritage from centuries of intermixing of European settlers with indigenous groups.

Martí's sentiments influenced many twentieth-century South American writers, including Borges in his attempt to grapple with what he saw as a Northern European tradition in contrast to the more indigenous heritage of his native Argentina. This struggle between north and south also affected artists such as the Uruguayan-Spanish Joaquín Torres-García (1874–1949). His deceptively simple drawing *América Invertida* (*Inverted America*, 1943) upends what was by then the widely accepted European version of maps placing north at the top, showing instead south as the prime direction, with the Equator and the latitudinal line running through Montevideo (which is depicted showing its exact coordinates). This inversion challenges the very notion of *South* America as a European colonial invention (symbolized by the sailing ship), while simultaneously trying to recover a southern identity using motifs drawn from pre-Columbian Meso-american cosmology. The Sun draws on the image of the Incan Sun god Father Inti, the Moon on the goddess Mama Quilla, while the fish is a symbol of fecundity.

1. The 'Blue Marble' photograph taken on NASA's Apollo 17 mission,
7 December 1972. On the left is the original image with south at the top.
On the right is the image released by NASA, with north at the top.

2. The 'Gasur map', a clay tablet from Yorgan Tepe, modern-day Iraq, showing cardinal directions, with east, or *IM-kur*, written in the top-left roundel, and west, or *IM-mar-tu*, bottom left. *c.* 2300 BCE.

3. A pre-Columbian Aztec codex depicting the cardinal directions, oriented with east (*tlapallan*) at the top, then moving clockwise, south (*huitzlampa*), west (*cihuatlampa*) and north (*mictlampa*).

4. The Tower of Winds, Athens, showing, from left to right, *Libs*, the south-west wind, *Notus* the south wind, and *Eurus*, the south-east wind. *c.* 100 BCE.

5. A Chinese compass (*luojing*) with its needle pointing south (*zhinan*).

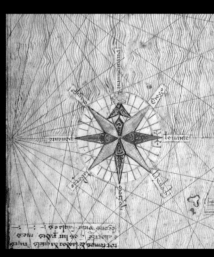

6. The first depiction of a compass rose, from Abraham Cresques' 'Catalan Atlas' (1375), using variants of the Latin terms for the eight directions, starting at the top going clockwise: *tramuntana* (north), *grego* (north-east), *levante* (east), *laxaloch* (south-east), *metzodi* (south), *libetzo* (south-west), *ponente* (west) and *magistro* (north-west).

7. Edmond Halley, 'A New and Correct Chart Showing the Variations of the Compass in the Western & Southern Oceans Observed in the year 1700 by his Majesty's Command' (1701), Royal Geographical Society.

8. A section from the Madaba Mosaic Map, Madaba Church, Jordan, showing Jerusalem. The map is oriented towards the east. Made with tesserae, *c.* 560 A D.

9. The first known twin hemispherical map, showing the western Spanish half of the globe and the eastern Portuguese half. Franciscus Monachus, *De orbis ac descriptio*, woodcut, 1524.

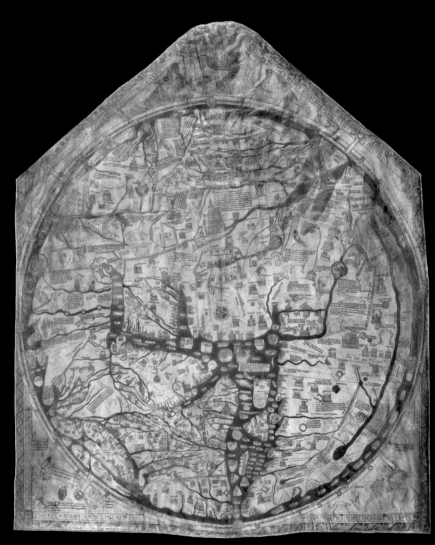

10. The Hereford *mappa-mundi*, with east and the Garden of Eden at the top, and south to the right, with its 'monstrous' races. Hereford Cathedral, *c.* 1300.

11. Cosmographical map of Egypt, oriented with Upper Egypt at the top, and south the cardinal direction. Stone sarcophagus, Saqqara, Thirtieth Dynasty, *c.* 350 BCE.

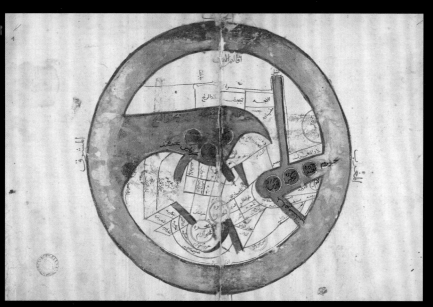

12. Copy of a lost world map by Muhammad al-Istakhri, 1297, centred on the Arabian peninsula and with south at the top.

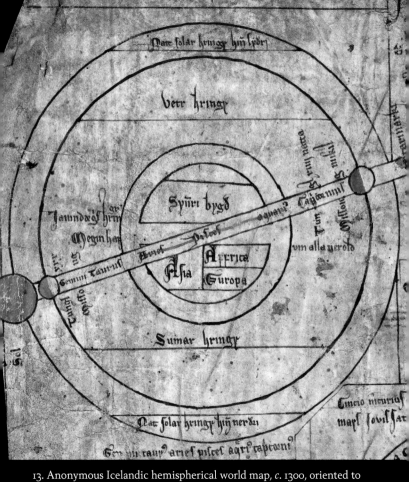

13. Anonymous Icelandic hemispherical world map, *c.* 1300, oriented to the south, with Asia to the left and Europe and Africa on the right

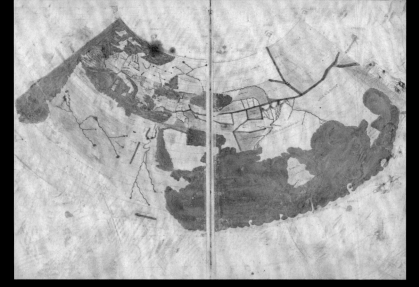

16: Anonymous Byzantine world map from one of the earliest copies of Ptolemy's *Geography*, thirteenth century, oriented to the north. Vatican Library.

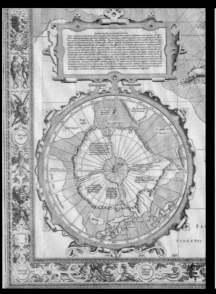

17. Gerard Mercator's world map (1569) putting north decisively at the top – though focusing on navigation

18. Frans Hogenberg's portrait of Gerard Mercator holding compass dividers over the North Pole, 1574.

19. The Selden Map, *c.* 1608–9, oriented with north at the top, depicting the earliest Chinese image of a compass rose.

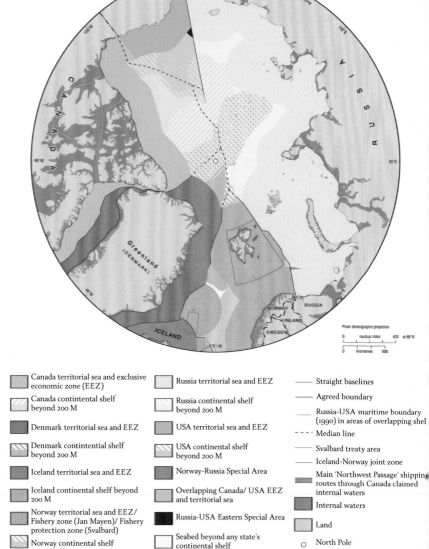

Canada territorial sea and exclusive economic zone (EEZ)

Canada continental shelf beyond 200 M

Denmark territorial sea and EEZ

Denmark continental shelf beyond 200 M

Iceland territorial sea and EEZ

Iceland continental shelf beyond 200 M

Norway territorial sea and EEZ/ Fishery zone (Jan Mayen)/ Fishery protection zone (Svalbard)

Norway continental shelf beyond 200 M

Russia territorial sea and EEZ

Russia continental shelf beyond 200 M

USA territorial sea and EEZ

USA continental shelf beyond 200 M

Norway-Russia Special Area

Overlapping Canada/ USA EEZ and territorial sea

Russia-USA Eastern Special Area

Seabed beyond any state's continental shelf

Straight baselines

Agreed boundary

Russia-USA maritime boundary (1990) in areas of overlapping shel

Median line

Svalbard treaty area

Iceland-Norway joint zone

Main 'Northwest Passage' shipping routes through Canada claimed internal waters

Internal waters

Land

North Pole

20. A 'Map of Maritime Jurisdiction and Boundaries in the Arctic Region', showing the countries laying claim to parts of the polar region, 2008.

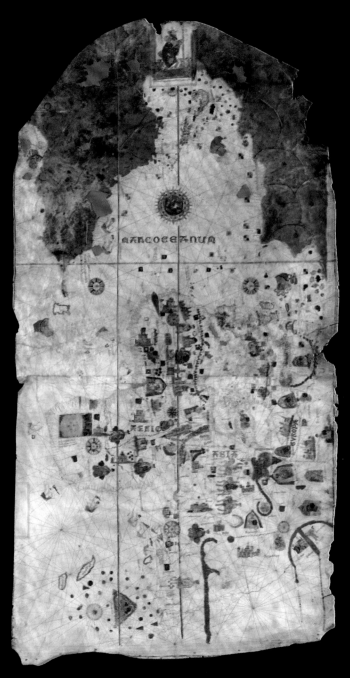

21. Juan de la Cosa, world map drawn in 1500, one of the only world maps to put west at the top. De la Cosa sailed with Columbus on his first voyage to the Americas in 1492.

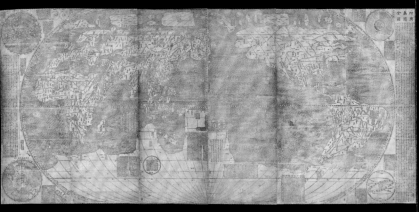

22. Matteo Ricci, Map of the World, with north at the top
and the 'Great West' to the left, including Europe, 1602.

23. Emanuel Leutze, *Westward the Course of Empire Takes its Way*, 1862.
Its central characters point west towards Oregon and California. Their
destination, San Francisco Bay, is shown at the bottom of the mural.

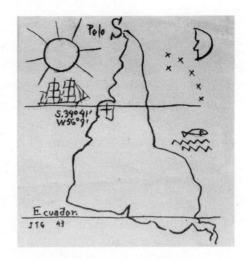

4. Joaquin Torres-García,
*Inverted America (América
Invertida)* 1943.

Torres-García's earlier manifesto *The School of the South* (1935)
had argued:

There should be no North for us, except in opposition to our
South.

That is why we now turn the map upside down, and now
we know what our true position is, and it is not the way the
rest of the world would like to have it ... When ships sail from
here travelling north, they will be travelling down, not up as
before. Because the North is now below. And as we face our
South, the east is to the left.

This is a necessary rectification; so that now we know
where we are.[20]

Here was a powerful response to the imposition of European
power, authority and belief across the continent stretching back
to Columbus's first landfall in 1492.

Others from the Antipodes took up Torres-García's challenge.
In 1979 the Australian map-maker Stuart McArthur produced
'McArthur's Universal Corrective Map of the World' (Plate 14).

79

Published on Australia Day on 26 January 1979, it places Australia at the top of the map next to a south-pointing compass drawing. McArthur had first drawn a version of the map in school and was told by his teacher to do it 'right' and put north at the top. The legend on the final published map includes the lines, 'No longer will the South wallow in a pit of insignificance, carrying the North on its shoulders for little or no recognition of her efforts. Finally, South emerges on top.' There is an alienating power to McArthur's ostensibly objective and scientific-looking map: when we turn anything the other way up it immediately looks different. Perhaps new patterns can be seen, or different connections between places. This was the charge of McArthur's reorientation. Ending 'Long live Australia – Ruler of the Universe!', the slightly tongue-in-cheek tone acknowledges that his task was still very much uphill.

But turning north and south upside down does not necessarily dismantle their power relations. In the decades of decolonization since Torres-García's challenge to the north, the south has continued to struggle with asserting an independent identity from Europe and the United States, both of which continue to exert significant influence on so much of the region's political and economic life. Even progressive attempts from the north to address the damage done to the south over the past 500 years have met with limited success. The political and economic language of international development in the 1970s took on a pronounced north–south preoccupation, delineated by the distinction between the undeveloped 'Global South' (first used in 1969), composed of Africa, Latin America and much of Asia, in contrast to the developed 'Global North', made up of the United States, Canada, Europe, parts of Asia, Australia and New Zealand. Again, this distinction is not based on strict geography but is more of a perception and an outlook, in this case based on relative economic prosperity.

It's All Gone South

A significant moment in the emergence of the 'Global South' came in 1980 with the publication of the Brandt Report. Chaired by the former Chancellor of West Germany, Willy Brandt, the report, entitled 'North–South: A Programme for Survival', aimed to challenge the geopolitical assumptions and hierarchies associated with 'First World' versus 'Third World' economic and social development and also to recalibrate the Cold War rhetoric of the time that divided the political world into the West, broadly understood as the USA and Europe, and the East, composed of the Soviet Bloc and China.[21]

In his introduction, Brandt characterized 'North–South relations as the great social challenge of our time'.[22] But, despite its good intentions, the report ran into difficulties from the outset. The first was its attempt to distinguish the economically developed North from the underdeveloped South. The report was published with a world map oriented with north at the top, across which was drawn the so-called 'Brandt Line'. The line ran from west to east, through Mexico, the Atlantic, North Africa, the Middle East, the then Soviet republics and China, before moving in a great loop to ensure Southeast Asia was placed in the south, with Australia and New Zealand in the north. It created a division that both utilized geography and ignored the latitudinal distinctions between north and south; the south was characterized as more of an idea than a place. The Brandt Line also seemed to underline rather than question the abiding power of Europe and North America to both orient the world according to its beliefs and draw lines across its surface.

Despite these problems of perception, the report acknowledged the North's domination of 'the international economic system, its rules and regulations, and its international institutions of trade money and finance', in contrast to an estimated 800 million people in the designated South living in absolute poverty. It argued that 'whatever their differences and however profound, there is a mutuality of interest between North and South. The fate of both is immediately connected. The search for solutions is not an act of benevolence but a condition of mutual survival.'[23] A large-scale redistribution of the North's wealth to the South – an estimated $4 billion per year over the following twenty years – would limit inflation, reduce future recessions and lead to global economic growth that would benefit both North and South.

The Brandt Report proposed an action plan based on addressing poverty, education, health, energy, gender inequality and reforms to the international economic system administered by the International Monetary Fund and World Bank. Such an ambitious and commendable project made claims that influenced the language and aspirations of much of the subsequent international development and aid policy of the North – a programme that is currently being challenged and rolled back by neo-liberal states across Europe and North America. The expression 'It's all gone south' is often used to describe something that has gone wrong and assumes that south is 'down', while north is 'up'. This certainly applies on more than one level to the Brandt Report, which foundered on the very North–South divisions it sought to address. Neither North nor South had enough cohesion or political will to implement its proposals. At the time of its publication the USA, Europe, China and Russia – all nominally part of the North – were in an East–West Cold War standoff that prevented any meaningful unity of action in relation to the South. Similarly, the South was fragmented across Latin American, African and Asian political organizations, many of which were openly antagonistic towards each other. Finally, as the report conceded from the outset, the South was neither homogeneous nor static, and by the 1990s the line defining it had predictably become blurred, with some countries in South America and Southeast Asia claiming economic parity with the North.

As Torres-García intimated in the 1930s, the South needed to speak back to the North rather than be spoken for, and in recent years this has started to happen, with the intervention of prominent activists and politicians from the Global South. They include Mia Mottley, Prime Minister of Barbados, who argued recently that the 'disparity between a handful of developed countries and the rest of the world is simply too shocking', and that 'the global south remains at the mercy of the global north' in matters of financial and environmental reform and equity.[24] Rather than assuming the Global South is trying but failing to play economic catch-up with the North, it is now at the forefront of many economic, political and economic developments in global capitalism.[25] Many activists and non-governmental organizations are fashioning their identities accordingly, with an acute sense of their geographical orientation. One such organization is #TheSouthAlsoKnows, a network of educational experts and decision-makers from South America, Asia, Africa and the Pacific who see themselves as Global Southerners, with a logo showing a south-oriented world map.

As the idea of the south has taken on greater range and complexity beyond its associations with frozen wastelands or exotic idylls, theatre has started to stage it in new and challenging ways. One of the most daring examples is the London-born Mojisola Adebayo's one-woman show *Moj of the Antarctic*, first performed in the capital in 2006. Adebayo uses the true story of the African-American Ellen Craft (1826–91) and her escape from slavery dressed as a white man to embark on an epic adventure as the first woman to reach Antarctica, including a lesbian love affair on the way. Like Torres-García, Adebayo wants to invert the long-held binary opposition between north and south from a different perspective, that of race, the history of the slave trade and life in southern plantations. As she reaches the 'black Antarctic mountain' set against shots of 'snow-topped land', Moj says:

> South to me was Georgia
> Now cotton has turned to snow
> In the deep deepest south of the earth.[26]

In the guise of 'the Ancient', a West African griot (storyteller), Adebayo reflects on distinctions between north and south:

> If Antarctica exists
> And the world is a wobbling wanderer
> Then nothing is straight
> And no one is straight
> Forward.
> If the world is a globe
> Then there is no above
> No below
> No North or South
> No heaven or hell
> No white or . . . (She prompts the audience to respond) black.
> No male or . . . (Prompting) female.[27]

If on a globe the cardinal directions are arbitrary, then aren't the national, racial and sexual distinctions that come with them also senseless?

*

As Adebayo's play shows, the old geopolitical assumptions characterized by the four directions on a magnetic compass are dissolving. Neither North nor West dominate; instead, the Global South offers a prime vantage point from which to view and understand the virtual, fluctuating identities and economies that structure so many aspects of modern economic and technological life. If this sounds far-fetched to readers in the North, they may be failing to understand the economic realities being forged in places like Lagos, Johannesburg, Jakarta and Manila. New developments in the liquid global economy, from its pursuit of state deregulation to outsourcing informal 'gig' economies, the rise of information technology services and the erosion of environmental controls, are all emerging in the South, not the North. The model of global capitalism that the South is driving is not necessarily progressive from a liberal perspective. It is just a different way of understanding our interconnected global world, for good and bad.

Such an approach does not reinstate an old geographical reality of the South. The 'Global South' is more of a relation than a location. This is why it includes so many regions usually categorized as 'eastern', including the maritime worlds of the Indian and Pacific oceans. But there is no such place as the 'Middle' or 'Far' South: in contrast to the East, the South is more of a frame of mind than a direction. It is now referred to by some anthropologists as 'an "ex-centric" location', embracing parts of South America, Africa and Asia.[28] Politically, expanding south-east political and economic alliances like BRICS (Brazil, Russia, India, China and South Africa) are reorienting the north-west alliance of the USA and Europe. Perhaps the South will end up turning the Western-dominated world upside down after all.

NORTH

Drawn North

North: the cardinal direction most consistently characterized as bleak, cold and dark, it is simultaneously a frozen wasteland of exile, punishment and death, filled with evil spirits, and the site of austere beauty, wonder, constancy, revelation, even salvation.[1] Yet, despite so many ambiguous, contradictory, even negative historical connotations, as we have seen, it sits at the top of nearly all modern maps.

The north is also one of the most powerful yet contradictory markers of personal identity: depending on where you live on the globe it can signify modernity and prosperity or poverty and backwardness. I am a northerner, but I am reluctant to accept that a term which over centuries has described the direction of winds and the point of a compass shapes who I am and how I speak and behave. Nevertheless, those who see themselves as northerners can hold powerful personal identifications – even pride – over and above those of the three other cardinal directions. Yet the presumptions of 'northernness' can flip and denote exactly the opposite depending on where you are. As noted in the first chapter, in Italy the stereotypical distinction between northerners and southerners is almost the exact opposite of that in England. Similarly, in the USA the north is regarded as politically and economically more developed in contrast to the conservative and rural south. Yet the meaning of being a 'northerner' can

also change across cultures. When I travel in the southern hemisphere I am no longer a 'northerner' but am labelled a 'westerner',
inhabiting different beliefs about the cardinal directions in relation to my personal identity.

As with all four cardinal directions, everything depends on
your location and use of 'geo-language' – the geographical situation and language you inhabit. In the case of the north, it is often
described as disappearing over the horizon, usually on a vertical
axis, something the poet Alexander Pope acknowledged in his
poem 'An Essay on Man' (1733–4) as he depicted an ever-receding
image of the north:

> Ask where's the North? at York, 'tis on the Tweed;
> In Scotland, at the Orcades; and there,
> At Greenland, Zembla, or the Lord knows where:
> No creature owns it in the first degree,
> But thinks his neighbour farther gone than he!

The Yorkshire-born poet Simon Armitage offers a similarly
wry perspective on the shifting boundary of the North in his
memoir *All Points North* (1998). For Armitage, the North 'can also
be Lancashire, which is really the North-West, and it can also be
Northumberland, which is the North-East, and sometimes it's
Humberside, which is the Netherlands, and it can be Cumbria,
which is the Lake District, and therefore Scotland'.[2] And these
north–south axes only multiply across the isles: Scotland sees
itself from the Outer Hebrides in the North Sea, while Wales
divides itself between the more authentically Welsh-speaking
north and the south viewed with suspicion as under the influence of the English (to the east).

But the north–south axis retains enduring characteristics
including simple assumptions such as 'up' (north) and 'down'
(south). This itself was shaped by a subtle shift in cardinal

directions over many centuries, as the north gradually displaced the east at the top of the map in most societies' literal and imaginative geography. But, before explaining why this might be, we need to understand the literal magnetism of the north.

North is distinguished among the four cardinal directions because of the peculiarity of the Earth's magnetic field. Geologists and astronomers know that rock types containing magnetite retain their original magnetic northern orientation when first formed, even if subsequently moved over millions of years. The rocks beneath our feet retain the signature of the north, and if, as some neuroscientists believe, animals' organelles also contain traces of magnetite (as noted in 'Orientation'), then much of our planet's mineral and organic fabric is hardwired to the north.

As a result, although the north postdates the axis of the east–west arc of the Sun identified by early societies, it nevertheless has come to exert a prime attraction, from climate and compasses to geographic poles and personal identification. We know that by the third century BCE Mesopotamian societies were orienting their maps with north (or more strictly north-west) as their cardinal direction, dictated by the direction of winds rather than astronomy, although sacred beliefs may also have played their part. Many of the communities living in the Fertile Crescent, including Persia, followed dualist spiritual beliefs, such as Manichaeism. Existence for them was driven by perennially opposing powers, elements and deities of light and dark, good and evil. In these world-schemes, light and spiritual revelation emanated somewhat surprisingly from the north. Manichaean thought developed an even more comprehensive cosmology in which the Tree of Life was to be found in the 'upper' part of the world to the north, while the Tree of Death was 'down' in the south. The Gnostic Mandaean sect of southern Mesopotamia that emerged in the first three centuries CE also developed a more astronomically driven reverence for the north, worshipping in the direction of the Pole Star as the source of light, constancy and healing.

Hyperborea

Other societies regarded the north more with fear and suspicion. Zoroastrians faced south to pray in the direction of the abode of Ahura Mazda, their creator deity. This was in direct contrast to the north, which they regarded as the domain of hell and the home of the female demon Druj Nasu, who travelled south to contaminate the bodies of the dead.[3] For the Zoroastrians, the north and its bitter winds were associated with death, evil, famine and sickness.

The ancient Chinese held deeply paradoxical ideas about the north. As we have seen, the celestial north held harmonious imperial associations, but its terrestrial version was a far more ambiguous place. The Han Dynasty court official and imperial jester Dongfang Shuo (c. 160–93 BCE) described a mythical 'journey to the North Pole' full of ghosts and illuminated by 'a blue dragon by means of a torch which it holds in its jaws'.[4] The 'Torch Dragon' – called *Zhuyin* or *Zhulong* – was a solar deity casting light into the darkness, a hallucinatory manifestation of the Aurora Borealis, or 'northern lights'. Tombs from the Shang Dynasty (c. 1760–1520 BCE) have revealed that elite burials were oriented to the north as the direction associated with illumination, but also death. A first-century BCE encyclopaedia advised burying the dead to the north of towns and cities, with the head of the deceased facing the same direction.[5]

The Greeks inherited a similar preoccupation with the north–south axis largely from Mesopotamian wind directions and subsequently astronomical observations. Ancient Greek cosmologies imply north (*Boreas*) was given precedence. In Aristotle's

Meteorology, 'up' and 'down' were equated with north and south. In describing the seas, Aristotle believed that as they 'flow down from high places, so in general the flow is greatest from the higher parts of the earth which lie towards the north'.[6] Although no world maps survive from the time, Aristotle's description of diagrams imagining the Earth's winds are all oriented with north at the top.[7] The assumption must be that whatever world maps were made by the Greeks, they were similarly oriented with north as the cardinal direction. Aristotle's pupil Dicaearchus of Messina (fl. c. 326–296 BCE) developed his master's diagrammatic descriptions with world maps (since lost) showing a parallel running east to west from Gibraltar to India, and a meridian running north to south through the Greek island of Rhodes. Within this scheme came the belief in the existence of a fertile land and blessed people in the northern extremes called 'Hyperboreans' (literally 'beyond the north wind'), a belief that went back at least as far as Homer. Not everyone was convinced. In his *Histories* Herodotus was sceptical about such people, invoking the Greek idea of global symmetry to argue, 'If there are Hyperboreans, there must be Hyperaustralians too', in the far south.[8]

Despite such suspicions, the view that the far north could embrace darkness and evil as well as peace and plenty would endure throughout time and across cultures in both hemispheres. Around 325 BCE, while Aristotle was conjuring the idea of *Boreas* in his *Meteorology*, the merchant and astronomer Pytheas of Massalia set sail from the Greek settlement in modern-day Marseilles in search of the north. Pytheas's lost treatise *On the Ocean* – which has been partially reconstructed from other sources – describes the earliest Greek voyage to the British Isles, the Baltic, and even possibly the Arctic Circle. His astronomical observations were the first to establish the position of the celestial pole directly above the imagined North Pole, and he also invented a new word for the world's end in the north:

'Thule'. Pytheas claimed Thule was six days' sail north of Britain, in a frozen sea. The word's origin is unknown – though it could relate to the Greek *telos*, or 'the end' – but in classical and medieval Latin *ultima Thule* came to describe the northernmost place in the world, variously identified as Iceland, Greenland, Norway or the Scottish Orkney Islands.[9]

Both the Pole Star and Thule were given their clearest definition by the Hellenic astronomer and geographer Claudius Ptolemy (Plate 16). His *Geography* (c. 150 CE) and *Almagest* (c. 169 CE) were the first texts to propose the position of Thule, which he claimed was an island off the coast of Scotland at the latitude of 63 degrees, and to identify correctly *Polaris* (the Pole Star) in his star catalogue. In the *Geography* Ptolemy provided detailed instructions for drawing a world map on a graticule – a grid of lines of latitude and longitude – with the meridians converging at an imaginary point above the North Pole at the top of the map. For Ptolemy, like earlier Greek scholars, geometry rather than theology established north as the prevailing cardinal direction, as can be seen in the earliest Byzantine copies of his *Geography*, which added the first world maps to the book, which were oriented to the north.

The naturalistic and scientific understanding of the north in Greek culture was rejected by Judaeo-Christian theology, which wanted to establish its monotheistic beliefs in contrast to what it saw as the 'pagan' beliefs of the Greeks and Romans. In Hebrew, the north, or *tsafon*, means 'hidden', as in the Sun, while the other term for north is *smol*, or 'left', indicating an enduring preference for east as the Jewish cardinal direction. Old Testament Scripture consequently described the north in primarily negative terms. In the Book of Ezekiel it is the direction of confusion and error. Ezekiel experiences a vision of God in Jerusalem who exhorts him: "'Son of man, look toward the north." So I looked, and in the entrance north of the gate of the altar I saw this idol of jealousy' (Ezekiel 8:5). The individuals, tribes or lands of Gog and Magog come from a 'place in the far north' (Ezekiel 38:14) at the end of days to battle with the Messiah, and feature throughout Abrahamic literature and maps. In the Book of Jeremiah the north is even more prophetic of disaster: 'Evil appeareth out of the north, and great destruction' (Jeremiah 6:1) is associated with the armies of King Nebuchadnezzar and the Babylonian destruction of Jerusalem. 'The Lord said unto me, "Out of the north an evil shall break forth upon all the inhabitants of the land"' (Jeremiah 1:13).

These negative connotations also affected Christian ritual and architecture. The north side of some medieval churches contains a 'Devil's Door', which was opened during baptism, while in others the Gospel was read on the altar's north side, both with the intention of expelling Satan's influence. The same side of the church was used to bury those who committed murder or suicide or were excommunicated.[10] Monsters and demons filled the frozen northern regions of medieval maps: the Hereford *mappa-mundi* described northerners as 'exceedingly savage people who eat human flesh and drink blood'. But, in keeping with the duality of perceptions of the north, it was also central to Creation according to the Book of Job, where God 'stretches out the north over empty space; He hangs the earth on nothing' (Job 26:7). It is also the direction from which salvation would come. In the Book of Job, Elihu prophesies that the 'awesome majesty' of God 'comes from the north as golden splendour' (Job 37:22). But old habits – and prime directions – die hard, and, even as Christianity took a right turn from classical culture to give east precedence over the north, the latter remained multivalent and proved hard to dislodge. Over time, the compass would eventually conquer Christ in returning north to the top of world maps.

North on Top

The simplest answer to why north came out on top is the convergence of two traditions. First, the classical Greek practice of using geometry to imagine and project the global Earth onto a two-dimensional plane surface put north on top, drawing on astronomical observations of the Pole Star and meteorological considerations of the winds privileging north. Second, the introduction of the magnetic compass as an aid to maritime navigation across the Mediterranean in the medieval period led first to sea charts, or 'portolans', and then most world maps being oriented to the north. This could have been due to taking bearings from magnetic north based on compass readings, but, as the Chinese knew, south would have worked just as well – by pointing due north a magnetized needle has necessarily also identified its opposite: due south. But the convergence of classical geometry and maritime navigational practice gave north a decisive edge over the other cardinal directions. Yet more prosaic factors also influenced its adoption, especially on many (though not all) portolan sailing charts. These charts were usually drawn on vellum, prepared using calfskin. To mimic the roughly oblong shape of the Mediterranean the neck of the flayed animal was usually positioned to the left, or west, on the map, which by default meant north was at the top. North had not necessarily supplanted the east in these charts, but they literally offered a new direction of travel.

As European powers colonized Africa, Asia and the Americas from the sixteenth century, indigenous mapping practices using cardinal directions other than north were erased or absorbed into a world picture with north at the top, dictated by Europeans at the expense of all other traditions. North – and by extension south – took on even sharper connotations as the former conquered the latter, creating both a directional and a cultural opposition. The logical consequence was that one direction (or culture) took precedence in all things and had to be 'on top' of the other. But the surviving evidence also suggests that 'the north' remained a troublesome term for many.

In Europe, the development of 'north' from the classical terms *boreas* and *septentriō* into the modern vernacular terms was a slow and contradictory process that also came with inauspicious connotations. Out of an estimated eighty Old English references to cardinal directions and their compounds, forty-eight used the emerging vernacular terms like *norþ* and *suð*, and thirty-two used the older Latinate terms. Yet 'north' also stems from the Sanskrit *narakah*, or 'hell', the ancient Greek *neretos*, 'lower' or 'nether world', and even the ancient Umbrian *nertru*, 'on the left' – of the Sun, while facing the east – with further associations of the spirits of the dead, from where we get the term Nerterology, or knowledge of the dead.[11]

The diffusion of these simpler terms across Europe was contradictory and uneven, with 'north' being the most equivocal of them. The ambiguity was compounded by the Renaissance rediscovery of classical Greco-Roman geography from the late fourteenth century. The most influential was Ptolemy's *Geography*, which became the cornerstone for European map-making. The data Ptolemy provided and inherited from earlier Greek thought indicate north was his prime orientation. European explorers like Columbus, da Gama and Magellan all used and accepted the northern orientation of Ptolemy's *Geography*, yet, even by the early sixteenth century, as their maps expanded in line with exploration, map-makers still offered a bewildering range of projections that were not exclusively oriented to the north. Some, like Giovanni Contarini's cordiform 1506 world map, looked like a cone or fan radiating outwards from the North Pole. Others were shaped like a heart (known as a cordiform projection), while the Italian Vesconte de Maggiolo's polar azimuthal projection could be centred on either pole. But none of these maps offered a definitive case for one cardinal direction, nor were they accurate enough to enable pilots to correctly calculate either the curvature of the Earth's surface or magnetic declination.

Nevertheless, assumptions about the fixed and constant nature of the northern Pole Star influenced medieval pilots in navigating according to its position. A typically elliptical reference to the constancy of the north appears in Shakespeare's *Hamlet* (1600). When teasing Rosencrantz and Guildenstern about his state of mind, Hamlet claims 'I am but mad north north-west'.[12] It's a riddle: a compass direction just 'off' north pointing NNW is only misaligned – or 'deranged' – for a moment and can quickly return to a 'constant' normal direction of 'true' north. But even here the shifting nature of astronomical observations – well known to the Elizabethans – meant that a consistent northern bearing was never fixed. When Alfred Hitchcock directed his classic spy thriller film *North by Northwest* in 1959, the title's reference to Hamlet was quite literally oblique. Hitchcock later said that 'the whole film is epitomized in the title – there is no such thing as north-by-north-west on the compass.'[13] The film's plot was originally conceived as moving in a north-westerly direction across the United States, from New York where it begins to Alaska, where Hitchcock first envisaged its denouement. The movie concludes in South Dakota, but Hitchcock's retention of the title reveals a director punning on his lack of control and true 'direction'.[14]

Squaring the Circle

The most compelling response to the problems of northern orientation had already emerged in 1569, when the Flemish geographer Gerard Mercator (1512–94) first published his celebrated world map using a projection subsequently named after him. The challenge that Mercator set himself was to create a map projection that could take into account magnetic declination and the curvature of the Earth's surface, allowing seaborne pilots to plot a straight line of bearing without gradually sailing way off course. In the map's address to the reader, Mercator described his famous solution to the problem as having 'progressively increased the degrees of latitude towards each pole in proportion to the lengthening of the parallels with reference to the equator'.[15] This effectively 'straightened' navigational lines of bearing plotted diagonally east to west for more accurate long-distance sailing, but it came at a cost: distortion of land mass increased the further away one travelled from the Equator, until the North Pole ran the full length of the map's top, as the South Pole did at its lower edge.

North was placed at the top of Mercator's map, following Ptolemy (Mercator would go on to produce his own edition of Ptolemy's *Geography* in 1578). But the north had a far greater significance for Mercator, one which has often been overlooked. In describing what he called the northern 'Septentrional Regions', Mercator wrote, 'as our chart cannot be extended as far as the pole, for the degrees of latitude would finally attain infinity, and as we yet have a considerable portion at the pole itself to present, we have deemed it necessary to repeat here the extremes of our representation and to join thereto the parts remaining to be represented as far as the pole.' To compensate for this maximal distortion at the North Pole, Mercator reproduced it on a much

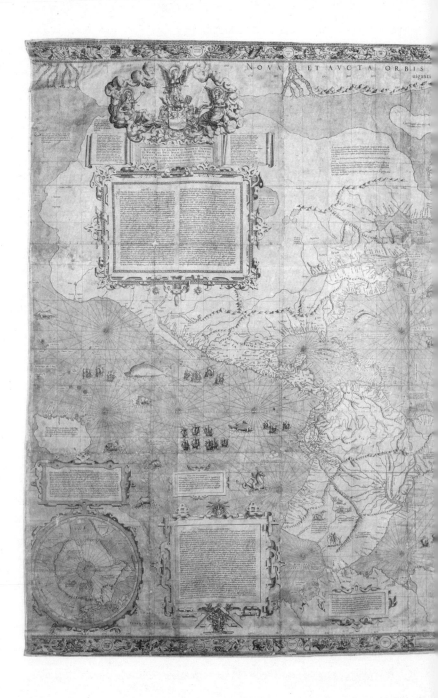

5. Gerard Mercator's world map (1569),
putting north decisively at the top – though
focusing on navigation east to west.

larger scale on the inset detail at the bottom left of the map, 'which is most apt for this part of the world and which would render the positions and aspects of the lands as they are on the sphere' (Plate 17). In this first detailed map of the region, Mercator was acknowledging that his world map for use in navigation could not properly represent the true nature of the North Pole, so he felt compelled to do so on the small inset map.

Mercator understood the problem for map-makers of the Earth's curvature and magnetic declination, both of which had frustrated accurate long-distance seaborne navigation for centuries. Pre-dating William Gilbert's explanation of the Earth as a giant magnet by thirty years, Mercator believed incorrectly that 'there must be a special pole towards which magnets turn in all parts of the world', and he tried to establish consistent variation 'common to the magnet and the world'. In doing so, he offered a fantastical account of the topography of the North Pole which came from obscure mythical accounts of an anonymous fourteenth-century English monk from Oxford who travelled into the Arctic region using his 'magical arts' to reach the land 'formerly called *Ciliae* (perhaps Thule), and now the Septentrionales'.[16] In Mercator's account based on the Oxford monk's, the region was surrounded by mountain ranges leading to four magnetic islands or 'countries' surrounding the pole. 'In the midst of the four countries is a whirlpool,' wrote Mercator, 'into which there empty these four indrawing seas which divide the North. And the water rushes round and descends into the Earth just as if one were pouring it through a filter funnel.' And 'right under the Pole lies a bare rock,' black and glistening, made of 'magnetic stone'. Not only did Mercator subscribe to a magnetic rock marking the North Pole: he also professed belief in a hollow Earth. In addition, he claimed that on one of the islands adjacent to the pole there 'live pygmies whose length in all is 4 feet, as are also those who are called Scraelingers in Greenland'.

Mercator's geography of the north may seem fantastical, but his approach was consistent not only with classical and medieval accounts of the region as filled with wondrous and monstrous people and places, but also with many of the previous descriptions of the South Pole. Where the south involved travelling inwards and downwards into the unconscious, Mercator's north involved probing into the inside of the skull represented as a globe. A portrait of Mercator by Frans Hogenberg, used to illustrate his later works, celebrates not Mercator's projection but his depiction of the North Pole (Plate 18). In his left hand he holds the globe while using his right hand to place dividers right over the North Pole, clearly showing the four islands surrounding the magnetic polar island, and a hollow Earth. One leg of the divider rests right next to the phrase 'Magnetic Pole'. Mercator looks like both a geographer surveying the globe and a physician about to plunge his medical callipers into the skull to find out what lies within and beneath the hollow cavity of the Earth (or mind). The north was thus both peripheral and central to Mercator's world map: absent in being projected to infinity in the main body of the map, but present in the detail of the North Pole in the bottom corner that revealed a world of Scraelingers, magnetic mountains and inflowing seas rushing in to the middle of the Earth.

Mercator's projection, with its attempt to calculate magnetic variation to the north, was eventually adopted by most state-sponsored voyages of exploration and colonization to the east and west of Europe over the next 400 years. It placed the north at the top of the world map, first those made in Europe and then – because of European domination – in the rest of the world, and this is where it has remained ever since. This was not based on Mercator's assumption of European supremacy as has sometimes been assumed. Ironically, north came at the top of his world map almost unintentionally because, in the sixteenth century at least, sailing there was almost impossible; it could therefore be projected to infinity without the need for it to be visited for any great length of time or colonized. What really mattered to the Christian imperial powers of the time was sailing with reasonable accuracy from west to east, along the trade routes of the Atlantic and Indian oceans, indicated by the ships covering Mercator's map. The European mercantile pre-occupation with east and west was paradoxically both served and reinforced by Mercator's iconic projection with north at the top.

Despite its obvious distortions and Mercator's opaque description of its mathematical formula, the projection gradually gained international success among those using maritime charts to such an extent that by the nineteenth century its origin hardly needed mentioning in the wall maps and educational atlases that incorporated it. Great Britain's Ordnance Survey adopted a version of it in 1938 as its default projection; the USA used the projection in their earliest satellite maps, and even utilized it in mapping the surface of Mars in the unmanned missions of the 1970s. Today, the Web Mercator Projection, a variant of the 1569 projection, is used by nearly all online mapping services, including Google, which adopted it in 2005. Its cardinal northern direction had triumphed almost inadvertently and is now being used to survey planets millions of kilometres beyond the one Mercator first mapped over 450 years ago.

Dark Materials

Even as Mercator was completing his projection, on the other side of the world, in Ming China, the north was also being cemented at the top of the world map, but for very different reasons, on a map of the Chinese mainland, the South China Sea and South-east Asia, known as the Selden Map of China. Named after the scholar John Selden (1584–1654), who bequeathed it to the Bodleian Library in Oxford, it is the earliest surviving Chinese map to show the whole of Southeast Asia and its maritime sea routes at a scale and in a style unknown in any comparable Asian map of the period (Plate 19). A Chinese map-maker made it some time in the first two decades of the seventeenth century, and it is now regarded as the most significant Chinese map of the last 700 years.[17]

Just a few decades after Mercator's projection, the Selden map also used north as its cardinal orientation, but not because of the magnetic pole. One of the map's unique features is its compass rose and scale bar, never seen on earlier Chinese maps. The compass rose has seventy-two points, with *luojing*, or 'compass', written in the middle. Chinese navigators had been using *luojing*, 'the thing that points south' (*zhinan*), since at least the tenth century. Some were dry-pivots (attached to a post), others involved placing a magnetized needle in water. Readings were used to draw up *zhenjing*, or 'compass manuals', the equivalent of European 'rutters', written descriptions of how to sail from one place to another based on compass readings. The *luojing* on the Selden map points south, but it is oriented with north at the top following the direction in which subjects faced their emperor.

But exactly what the north represented for Chinese and other Asian societies remained complex and contradictory. In Chinese dynastic thought, the north took on more specific geographical dimensions as a threatening place, a wasteland beyond the Great Wall, the home of savage invaders marking the line between (southern) civilization and (northern) barbarism. In eighth-century Chinese poetry any place north of the Great Wall was imagined as the end of the world. In the poem 'On the Frontier' by Li He (791–816 CE), an invading army beyond the wall brings with it an apocalyptic image of the direction it represents: 'North of their tents is surely the sky's end.'[18] The most dangerous enemies came out of the north. This explains the geo-strategic positioning of Beijing as the imperial capital city in the fifteenth century – in the north, to ensure military capacity was concentrated there to prevent Mongol invasions. The Chinese term for the Forbidden City is Zijincheng: *jin* means forbidden, *cheng* refers to a walled fortress and *zi* means purple – the colour associated with the North Star and the abode of the mythical Jade Emperor. Mixing barbaric invaders with ghosts, ice and darkness, the north has remained a perennially threatening yet evocative place in the Chinese imagination, even adopted to describe Mao Zedong's famed Long March to the North (1934–5), which became mythologized as the beginning of his rise to power within the Chinese Communist Party.

Japanese culture inherited similarly ambivalent approaches to the north (*kita*) alongside its opposite, south (*minami*), with north-east (*kimon*) regarded as the most inauspicious direction, literally translated as the 'demon gate'. Traditional Japanese homes were designed in accordance with the proper alignment of cardinal directions, especially north.[19] In 1689 the Edo poet Matsuo Bashō (1644–94) set off northwards from Edo (Tokyo) through the mountains in a journey that would eventually lead him to the largely unexplored regions around Ōgaki. For Bashō, the journey to the north – or the limits of what is known – was a metaphor for life itself: *Oku no Hosomichi*, often translated as his book's more familiar title, *The Narrow Road to the Deep North*.

Bashō's metaphorical journey north involved travelling into the 'interior' of his mind. Such northern extremities also inspired subsequent European writers. The beginning of the English literary tradition of imagining the northern polar regions starts with Mary Shelley's *Frankenstein* (1818). The novel is written in the form of a series of letters composed 'far north of London' by Captain Robert Walton to his sister. They are written first from St Petersburg and then Archangel as he travels northwards 'on a voyage of discovery towards the northern pole', which he describes as a 'region of beauty and delight'. The story of Frankenstein's creation is subsequently told through flashback, as the monstrous creature torments his creator and lures him towards 'the everlasting ices of the north'. When Frankenstein dies he promises Walton he will 'seek the most northern extremity of the globe', where he will end his life. The novel ends with the creature leaping onto an ice raft heading north, 'borne away by the waves and lost in darkness and distance'. Walton's pursuit of the north – a place he blithely and wrongly believes is uninhabited – is as misguided and hubristic as Frankenstein's creation.[20]

Most recently, Philip Pullman's *His Dark Materials* trilogy (1995–2000) included the *Northern Lights* (1995), in which a parallel Arctic 'North' is the scene for the hero Lyra Belacqua's quest to find missing friends and family. Lyra's first sight of the Aurora Borealis suggests a world beyond hers and is the 'magnet' that drives her journey. Her travels northwards from Oxford and London's imaginary Arctic Institute involve using an alethiometer, Pullman's imagined device for symbolic wayfinding and the inner truth, described as 'very like a clock, or a compass, for there were hands pointing to places around the dial, but instead of the hours or the points of the compass there were several little pictures'.[21]

White Light

From Bashō to Pullman, Asian and European literary depictions of the Arctic had one thing in common: the omission of the indigenous people who lived there. Encompassing around 15 per cent of the Earth's land surface, the Arctic is home to the Inuit, the Aleuts, the Saami and various other groups in the North American Arctic and northern Russian territories.[22] The Inuit, with a current population of around 150,000, inhabit land adjoining three oceans (Atlantic, Arctic and Pacific), running from the 55th parallel north on the Labrador Coast in modern Canada to 80 degrees north in Greenland. They were largely insulated from the initial depredations of European colonization that decimated the Americas following Columbus's arrival. The Arctic region was deemed too environmentally hostile and lacking in recognized trade goods to be of interest to European colonizers. But by the nineteenth century whaling and fur trading brought *qallunaat*, the Inuit word for white people, to the region in significant numbers. Estimates indicate that in the nineteenth century the indigenous populations in some parts of Alaska and north-western Siberia dropped by 50–85 per cent due to the impact of European disease and competition for natural resources.[23]

On 1 June 1831 the English naval officer James Clark Ross reached the north magnetic pole on the Boothia Peninsula in northern Canada, claiming it for the English Crown. It was something of a hollow claim, as the position of the magnetic pole shifts around 40 kilometres a year. Using their magnetic compasses to reach the ultimate point of their version of north, European explorers like Ross discovered that the Inuit neither recognized the concept of north nor saw themselves as 'northerners'. The Pole star did not possess the metaphysical significance for the Inuit that it held for those living in lower European latitudes. There was a simple reason for this: above 68° N the star appeared too high in the sky to be practical as a navigational point of bearing, especially when driving a dog team in poor weather and limited visibility. Inuit communities in the latitudes of north-western Greenland did not even have a name for the star. Those from more southerly places used various terms for it, but none were particularly fixed or stable. Some called it *Nuuttuit-tuq*, meaning 'never moving', *Turaagaq*, 'something to aim at', or occasionally *Ulluriaqjuaq*, 'great star'.[24]

The Inuit had to develop other wayfinding methods with little or no recourse to stars or magnetic compasses. In the 1980s the anthropologist John MacDonald interviewed Inuit travellers in Igloolik while writing the first English-language book on their astronomical beliefs and navigational practices. One of the Igloolik community, Aipilik Innuksuk, told him, 'some people get lost when they used only the skies for navigation and did not pay attention to the ground. They would get lost because the stars are continually moving ... That is why I have to be aware of the ground.'[25] MacDonald noted that the word the Inuit used for such awareness of where they were regardless of conditions was *aanqaittuq*, or 'ultra-observant'. Its opposite was *aangajug*, translated as someone who 'moves away from the community and immediately loses where his destination is at, so as a result will travel blindly'.[26] To 'blind' European travellers using scientific navigational instruments such as the magnetic compass, the Arctic appeared to be a wasteland, a featureless space devoid of life. Here was a region populated by people who were either ignored or co-opted as aesthetic props in the Romantic creation of what has been called 'the Arctic sublime'.[27]

The pursuit of the ultimate northern point on the globe brought its own, more self-inflicted casualties among European explorers. The most famous of all was Sir John Franklin. In May 1845 Franklin left England with two ships and a crew of 128. It is often assumed Franklin was intent on finding a northwest passage between the Atlantic and Pacific oceans through the Arctic Ocean. In fact, Franklin had accepted many years before that even if such a passage existed it would be commercially useless. Following the discovery of the magnetic north by his friend Captain James Clark Ross in 1831, Franklin proposed a return voyage to conduct six months of magnetic observations. He planned to compile geomagnetic charts that would accurately predict the Earth's magnetic field. The ships were named the *Terror* and *Erebus* (the Greek deity personifying darkness and chaos and the place of the dead in the underworld). Trapped in the ice off King William Island in the Canadian Arctic Archipelago, Franklin's ships were last spotted in July 1845. It seems Franklin struggled on but died sometime in June 1847. The rest of the crew continued to try to find a way out of the ice, and may have resorted to cannibalism before they finally succumbed to hypothermia and starvation.

Franklin's death in pursuit of the magnetic north sent shockwaves through Victorian England. His widow, Lady Franklin, imposed the grander myth of her husband as a heroic explorer pursuing the north-west passage. Alfred, Lord Tennyson wrote his epitaph, registering the national trauma of Franklin's loss to the icy north, and his voyage beyond the poles into the afterlife:

Not here! The white North has thy bones; and thou,
Heroic sailor-soul,
Art passing on thine happier voyage now
Toward no earthly pole.[28]

The 'white North' had claimed Franklin, just as 'the great white desert' of the South would claim Captain Scott sixty-five years later.

White Race

The Victorians' fascination with the 'old north' of Vikings, Iceland and Norway, and its 'white' ethnic purity, went hand in hand with the imperial ideology of the 'White Man's Burden' – Europe and America's moral obligation to explore, colonize and bring civilization and 'progress' to the non-white world. It spawned twentieth-century racial fantasies of the 'Nordic race' as a superior group, colonizing and conquering all four points of the compass.[29] The term 'race nordique' was first coined in 1900 by the Russian anthropologist Joseph Deniker, and it quickly became associated with the language of Aryan, Teutonic and Anglo-Saxon pseudo-scientific racism that came to – and still continues to – underpin fascist regimes including the Nazis in their pursuit of a white, northern 'master race'.[30]

Towards the end of the nineteenth century the United States also joined in the race to discover what became known among competing explorers as 'Farthest North', a pursuit imbued with racism and misogyny. As the search for a north-west passage waned, the pursuit of the North Pole as an end in itself intensified as British and American male explorers vied for the imperial kudos of getting there first. Throughout the 1890s the race was led by the US explorer and naval officer Robert Peary, in search of what he called 'the great white mystery of the North'.[31] Between 1886 and 1909 Peary led eight expeditions to the Arctic, crisscrossing Greenland and drawing on Inuit local knowledge to move ever closer to what he believed to be the exact location of the North Pole. Writing an essay on 'The Lure of the North Pole' in 1906, Peary described it in terms that echoed the philosophical and poetic descriptions stretching back to the ancient Greeks. 'The North Pole is the precise centre of the Northern Hemisphere, the hemisphere of land, of population, of civilization,' he wrote:

It is the point where the axis of the Earth cuts its surface. It is the spot where there is no longitude, no time, no north, no east, no west – only south; the place where every wind that blows is a south wind. It is the place where there is but one night and one day in every year – where two steps only separate astronomical noon from astronomical midnight. The spot from which all the heavenly bodies appear to move in horizontal courses, and a star just visible above the horizon never sets, but circles for ever, just grazing the horizon.[32]

For Peary, the pole was ultimate north, the top of the world, just waiting to be claimed by a 'civilized' white man. This was 'the last great geographical prize which the world has to offer . . . for which the best men of the strongest, most enlightened, most adventurous nations of the Earth have been struggling unsuccessfully for nearly four centuries: the trophy which the grandest nation of them all would be proud to win.'[33]

Peary's final push to the north began in July 1908, when he left New York on board the *Roosevelt*. The crew included Matthew Henson, an African American sales clerk who had travelled with Peary on all his Arctic expeditions since 1887. Hiring several Inuit guides and dog sledges on their arrival in Greenland in February 1909, the expedition made its way north. On 6 April Peary used a sextant to take measurements of the Sun's angle and estimated his latitude to be 89°57'. He claimed his readings were taken 'over or very near the point where north and south and east and west blend into one'.[34] Peary was convinced he was as close to the pole as possible based on modern scientific estimates, and could now claim it as 'his'. Henson was tasked with scouting ahead of Peary's last readings and returned saying, 'I think I'm the first man to sit on top of the world.' Peary was furious, took further readings, decided that Henson was still five kilometres from the pole and set off to plant his flag. He had fulfilled what he always regarded as his and America's destiny in Greenland: 'the Stars and Stripes wrested its savage northern headland out of the mist and gloom of the Polar night.' Henson's claim was quietly forgotten.

Orientation may have collapsed at the pole, but Peary ensured that prevailing imperial racial hierarchies were reinforced. He had already imagined the order of things when he finally reached the

6. Photograph of Matthew Henson and four Inuit guides, Ooqeah, Ootah, Egingwah and Seeglo, taken by Robert Peary at what he believed to be the North Pole, April 1909.

northern summit. 'There, on that most northern land,' he wrote, 'the most northerly known fixed point on the face of the Earth, never trodden before perhaps by human foot, were gathered the representatives of three great races – myself the Caucasian, Henson the Ethiopian, Anghmaloktok the Mongolian'.[35] In this bizarre racial model, Peary, the white 'Caucasian', returned to classical Greco-Roman categories, with Henson transformed into an 'Ethiopian' and the Inuit guide Anghmaloktok turned into a 'Mongolian'.

Reaching somewhere that approximated to the North Pole was one thing: having it accepted by the rest of the world was another. Upon his return to the United States in the autumn of 1909, Peary was busy trying to write Henson's claim out of history when he learned that the explorer Frederick Cook was claiming to have reached the North Pole a year earlier, in April 1908. Like Peary, Cook – a former surgeon on one of Peary's earlier expeditions – described the quasi-mystical 'commanding call of the Northland. To invade the Unknown, to assail the fastness of the white frozen North', what he called the 'boreal centre'.[36] But upon his arrival at what he believed was the pole, Cook experienced a profound sense of elation, then deflation. 'North, east, and west had vanished. It was south in every direction, but the compass pointing to the magnetic pole was as useful as ever,' he wrote. But then, 'though overjoyed with the success of the conquest, our spirits began to descend on the following day ... what a cheerless spot to have aroused the ambition of man for so many ages! An endless field of purple snows. No Life. No land ... We were the only pulsating creatures in a dead world of ice.'[37]

As there was no definitive physical landmark or objective scientific method for determining the exact point of the geographic North Pole, both men stood by their claims to precedence, with neither capable of producing definitive and independently verifiable evidence to support their case. The US House of Representatives became involved and backed Peary, as much on political as scientific grounds. The Royal Geographical Society also certified Peary's claim and awarded him its prestigious gold medal in 1910, but its members were split over the decision, and to this day doubts still linger over who has the best claim to coming closest to standing first on the imaginary pole. Geographically and scientifically speaking, the north had no enduring physical point – perhaps what drove Cook's disappointment in reaching something that wasn't really there. The north continues to move and shift due to physical and geomagnetic forces. Like its Antarctic opposite, there is no definitive 'there' there.

In recent years black artists have started to challenge the white, male racial fantasies of the North Pole like Peary's to reimagine it as both a place and an idea. In his large-scale multiple-screen video installation *True North* (2004), the black British installation artist and filmmaker Isaac Julien revisualizes the Arctic and its 'discovery' by Henson. It retells the expedition's story from Henson's perspective, using his memoir, *A Negro Explorer at the North Pole* (1912), and images of their four largely forgotten Inuit guides. Henson wrote that when Peary raised the US flag over the pole he 'felt a savage joy and exultation. Another world's accomplishment was done and finished. And as in the past, from the beginning of history, wherever the world's work was done by a white man, he had been accompanied by a colored man.'[38] Julien uses Henson's words to 'reorient' the usual story of polar exploration as one of physical and racial whiteness. His title even plays on different symbolic meanings that 'north' – and south – would have for a descendant of black slaves like Henson, whose parents were free Black American sharecroppers. As Robert Stepto has argued, 'the seminal journey in Afro-American narrative literature is unquestionably north,'[39] from the slavery of the southern plantation states to the relative freedom of the north. Henson had experienced first-hand the racist assumptions and climate determinism of the Antebellum South of the United States that claimed black people could not move north but should stay in the 'tropical' south. On his return in 1909, Henson announced, 'When I went to Greenland they said I would never come back. They told me that I could not stand the cold – and no black man could. I said I would die if necessary to show them. I survived all right and here I am.'[40]

The London-born theatre artist Mojisola Adebayo took Julien's reimagination of the black presence at the North Pole even further in *Matt Henson, North Star* (2009), a northern companion to her earlier reflections on the South Pole, *Moj of the Antarctic*. Adebayo's central character encounters various real and historical figures, including an Inuit woman called Akat-ingwah and Peary himself. Henson holds Peary to account for marginalizing him from the 'discovery' of the pole until 'the geography of his body disappeared from the map'. But Akat-ingwah also challenges Henson for his complicity in the death, chaos and destruction he and Peary brought to the Inuit (includ-ing the abandonment of their mixed-race offspring). Henson responds angrily, 'the North Pole is the greatest discovery since the new world! I am descended from southern slaves and I have ascended to the summit of the planet – an African at the apex of the earth! You should be proud of me . . . This isn't what I want told. I'm the kind one. I'm the victim in all this.' Both men – one black, one white – conspire in the oppression of Inuit women in the north. The play ends with Peary offering a new direction: 'let us turn our faces South, toward the future.'[41]

Nordicity

The decline of European and American imperial exploration and the advent of decolonization in the twentieth century also brought a more reflective attitude to the North that began to appear in Europe to challenge the racist fantasies of Nordic 'superiority'. The Victorian mythology of the North inspired by Franklin's disappearance remained, yet English poets – many from the north of England – imagined a purer, redemptive version of the cardinal direction. The British poet W. H. Auden – born in York but raised in the Midlands – traced much of his poetic inspiration back to the north. 'My feelings have been oriented by the compass as far back as I can remember,' he wrote in a maga-zine article playfully entitled 'I Like it Cold', published in 1947. 'Though I was brought up on both, Norse mythology has always appealed to me infinitely more than Greek . . . Years before I ever went there, the north of England was the Never-Never Land of my dreams. Nor did those feelings disappear when I finally did; to this day Crewe railway junction marks the wildly exciting frontier where the alien South ends and the North, my world, begins.'[42]

Auden's spiritual orientation allowed him to create his own interior world of directional associations:

North and South are the *foci* of two sharply contrasted clusters of images and emotions . . . North – cold, wind, precipices, glaciers, caves, heroic conquest of dangerous obstacles, whales, hot meat and vegetables, concentration and production, privacy. South – heat, light, drought, calm, agricultural plains, trees, rotarian crowds, the life of ignoble ease, spiders, fruits and desserts, the waste of time, publicity.[43]

Auden wanted to create a different aesthetic from the prevailing classical 'southern' tradition he inherited as an English poet. So instead he embraced the language of Old English, or what he called 'the "barbaric" poetry of the North'.[44]

As Auden was reimagining a mythical North, English-speaking and francophone writers and thinkers were providing more political responses to the long history of colonial violence and settlement from and within places designated north. In 'North', a poem published in a collection of the same title at the height of the Troubles in his native Northern Ireland in 1975, Seamus Heaney reflected on the long complex history of northernness. Looking northwards from the Donegal coast, Heaney imagined the 'powers of the Atlantic thundering', the 'fabulous raiders' – Vikings – bringing a contradictory heritage of 'geography and trade', 'spilled blood' and a 'word hoard'. From such a complex history and geography, Heaney realizes he will have to '[c]ompose in darkness', and '[e]xpect aurora borealis' – moments of dark poetic insight – 'but no cascade of light'.[45]

While Heaney used poetry to understand the deep historical reasons for the violence and sectarian conflict engulfing his homeland, Canada's social scientists were also revising social and political attitudes towards its so-called northern territories and their indigenous communities. Whereas its southern neighbour the United States understood itself as part of an east–west axis shaped by the imaginative power of its western frontier (as we shall see in the next chapter), Canada imagines itself north to south, sandwiched between the US to the south and the Arctic territories to the north. The Northwest Territories, Nunavut and Yukon together comprise 40 per cent of the country's land mass, yet only 1 per cent of the population live there. In the 1960s, in an attempt to address these ethnic and geographical inequalities, Canadian geographer Louis-Edmond Hamelin drew up what he called a polar or 'Global Nordic Index'.[46]

Like Heaney, Hamelin wanted to push back on the late nineteenth- and early twentieth-century biological racism of Nordicity as an index of white supremacy. Instead, Hamelin's Index defined 'Nordicity' as 'a state or level of northernness' based on ten quantifiable elements, ranging from latitude, climate and vegetation, to economic activity and living conditions, each being scored from 0 to 100. His Index identified about 70 per cent of Canada's territory as Nordic (as opposed to the official estimate of 39 per cent), more extensive than Scandinavia or even Siberia, a fact that discouraged settlement and economic development in tandem with the lived experience of indigenous communities. Hamelin's Index allowed state support for economic and social services to enable these isolated 'northern' regions – that Hamelin divided up into what he called 'isonords' – to remain in contact with the South.[47]

One of the most eloquent and enigmatic responses to the changing perceptions of the Canadian north came from the Canadian pianist Glenn Gould in his experimental radio documentary 'The Idea of North' (1967). Bringing together a group of Canadian men and women with experience of the northern territories, the documentary recreated a train journey aboard the 'Muskeg Express', from Winnipeg to Churchill, an Arctic port in northern Manitoba, a distance of 1,700 kilometres that takes over two days to complete. Introducing the documentary, Gould admitted that he 'had no real experience of the North'. Instead it remained 'a convenient place to dream about, spin tall tales about, and, in the end, avoid'.[48]

Gould wove together what he called a 'contrapuntal' soundscape of voices expressing different experiences of the northern territories. In Gould's documentary there are three main voices: a government official called Bob Phillips, a geographer called Jim Lotz and a nurse called Marianne Schroeder. As the train clatters northwards, Bob Phillips acknowledges the colonial history of the northern territories and how Canadians were 'supremely oblivious to the responsibilities we had to the people there . . . we just didn't care about the North. It was a great sort of *terra nullius*.' In capturing the destructive assumptions made by Europeans throughout the nineteenth century in their pursuit of the north, Phillips concluded 'there's a lot in that Romantic tradition that in my mind was pretty ugly judged by today's standards.' The geographer Jim Lotz agreed with Phillips, reflecting that 'in the North, in many respects we're at our sort of greatest, and our most grotesque.'

There was no space in Gould's documentary for the presence or voices of the indigenous communities simply labelled 'northerners' or 'Eskimos' or women's voices, aside from Marianne Schroeder, who recounts people telling her they 'didn't think it was a country for a woman . . . trying to face the world by herself'.

In 1995 the Canadian novelist Margaret Atwood addressed these absences in *Strange Things: The Malevolent North in Canadian Literature*. Atwood claimed that 'Canadians have long taken the North for granted, and we've invested a large percentage of our feelings about identity and belonging in it.'[49] Addressing fictional responses to the north, Atwood observed that in most male Canadian writing, the north functions as a wilderness and a frontier, a physical place and a state of mind. It 'was uncanny, awe-inspiring in an almost religious way, hostile to white men, but alluring; that it would lead you on and do you in; that it would drive you crazy, and, finally would claim you for its own'.[50]

The fear of madness and destruction confronted at the furthest points of each cardinal direction have often appeared in the form of monsters. Medieval *mappae-mundi* depicted the monstrous races at its southern extremities. In Canada, as Atwood points out, such fears appear from the north in a very specific monstrous shape: the Wendigo (also known as 'Windigo', 'Wetiko' and various other Algonquian names). The Wendigo 'is a spirit creature with a heart and sometimes an entire body of ice'. It can murder and eat people as well as possessing them, transmitting an insatiable hunger for human flesh. The Wendigo has its origins in the folk traditions of the northern American Algonquian-speaking people, including the Ojibwe, who call it *wiindigoo*. Jesuit missionaries first encountered stories of the Wendigo near Quebec in the early seventeenth century, where it often appeared as the personification of the north and its defining characteristics: cold, darkness and starvation.

From the nineteenth century the Wendigo permeated Canadian settler writing and was a recurrent characteristic of the dangers – and perhaps deeply buried pleasures – of what happens when you go too far into the north. Driven to extremes of human solitude and physical deprivation, the north could send you mad or, in the parlance of early Canadian settlement, lead to 'cabin fever' or becoming 'bushed'. In seeking to transform themselves by pushing the limits of their physical endurance, European settlers could embrace – and perhaps invited – their loss of self. As Atwood puts it in identifying the fears and desires surrounding becoming Wendigo, 'the desire to be superhuman results in the loss of whatever small amount of humanity you may still retain.'[51]

In the 1920s 'Wendigo psychosis' even became a clinically recognized form of insanity where patients felt possessed by cannibalistic obsessions.[52] Although more recently discredited by the psychiatric community, the myth of the Wendigo as a terrifying result of contact between Europeans and indigenous communities in the north retains a strong hold on the popular imagination. While psychiatry may have distanced itself from Wendigo psychoses, historians have taken up some of its dimensions in exploring the psychological dynamics of colonial power. In 1978 Jack D. Forbes, a First Nations writer and activist of Algonquian heritage, published *Columbus and the Cannibals: The Wétiko Disease of Exploitation, Terrorism and Disease*.[53] For Forbes, 'imperialism and exploitation are forms of cannibalism' in its metaphorical sense of 'the consuming of another's life for one's own purpose or profit'. The arrival of Columbus in 1492 brought with it what Forbes called 'the *wétiko* disease, the sickness of exploitation'. Europeans had 'consumed' the indigenous communities, appropriating their land and resources and enslaving them in a murderous ritual of cannibalistic 'self-serving consumption'. As far as Forbes was concerned, the *wétiko* from the north was a symbol of the European sickness of colonial enrichment, feeding off indigenous people.

Throughout nineteenth-century writing – almost exclusively male – Atwood noticed a recurrent trope: that 'the North is a cold *femme fatale* enticing you to destruction'. But by the mid-twentieth century women writers started to take a different direction. Atwood noticed that 'instead of going off into the woods to be with a man, they start going off into the woods to be by themselves. And sometimes they're even doing it to get *away* from a man.'[54] In Marian Engel's novel *Bear* (1976) a librarian called Lou travels to north-eastern Ontario where she develops a sexual relationship with a bear. For Atwood, the story of a woman's encounter with this furry symbol of the north rewrites the typical male story. 'She does not conquer the natural world, or penetrate it,' writes Atwood. Instead, 'she befriends it'.

While this shift in understanding the north may represent a break from the dominant male desire to romanticize, conquer and dominate it, Atwood is too astute to celebrate, warning 'the bad news is coming in: the North is not endless'. Environmental pollution and climate change are taking their toll on the region and the people who live there. Without action, Atwood warns that 'the North will be neither female nor male, neither fearful nor health-giving, because it will be dead.'[55]

The Death of the North

As the polar ice melts and sea levels rise, geopolitical debates over what constitutes the northern polar region have emerged as nations assess the gas, oil and mineral wealth that new technology could potentially extract from the region. In 2007 Russian marine scientists dived over 4,000 metres and claimed 'the Arctic is Russian' by planting a titanium flag on the Lomonosov Ridge situated between the New Siberian Islands and the Canadian Arctic Archipelago. The International Boundaries Research Institute (IBRU) based at Durham University subsequently published the first of a series of 'Arctic Maps' (Plate 20). These were commissioned by the United Nations' Division for Ocean Affairs and the Law of the Sea for its 'Commission on the Limits of the Continental Shelf' (CLCS) to address the competing claims to the Arctic regions from six states (Canada, Denmark, Iceland, Norway, Russia, USA). In trying to resolve these claims and disputes, the map demarcates and apportions rivers, seas and economic zones between the six claimants.

It is one of the many paradoxes of the north that the region regarded as virtually unmappable on Mercator's world projection, and for most of human history impassable due to ice, should now be the site of a political battle. As ecological change transforms the region's land and waterways, the long-held fantasies of establishing north-west and north-east maritime passages across and through the Arctic could become a dramatic reality. The world is entering a political 'cold rush' to claim and extract the region's previously inaccessible oil, gas and mineral reserves, despite repeated warnings from activists and writers about the catastrophe that would be triggered by trying to plunder these reserves. Atwood's warning is stark: 'The Earth, like trees, dies from the top down. The things that are killing the North will kill, if left unchecked, everything else.'[56]

The North's future is now focused not just on its topography, but on the very real possibility that climate change could mean that what is understood as the north might not exist in a few years. In his book *A Farewell to Ice*, the sea-ice scientist Peter Wadhams explains in terrifying detail how the data describing what is known as the 'Arctic Death Spiral' reveals 'that the summer Arctic sea ice does not have long to live'.[57] The disappearance of this ice means that the north-east passage north of Russia, now known as the Northern Sea Route (NSR), will soon become regularly ice-free, enabling shipping and mineral exploration to flourish and accelerate global warming. Before long the summer months will see the Arctic free of ice, creating a devastating albedo effect. Summer sea ice reflects 50 per cent of incoming radiation back into space. Its disappearance will cause an albedo-driven warming across the Arctic and the rest of the planet. The results will be catastrophic. Wadhams predicts that 'it will not just be farewell to ice, but farewell to life.'[58] The north and its polar region, inextricably connected to the magnetic core of the planet, is the most in danger of being erased by human greed and ignorance, driven primarily by the economic policies of the Global North.

WEST

Rise and Fall

West is where the day comes to an end, the Sun sets, night draws in and the story told in this book comes to a close. Like its opposite, the east, the west is defined by the passage of time rather than space, but with a very different trajectory. The western sunset personifies the conclusion of time with the end of life's heliocentric journey and it anticipates the terrors of the night, darkness and death. Where the story of time begins in the east, the west comes with a sense of its ending. In Japanese, *nishi* is the west, synonymous with what is past.[1] As a result, no premodern societies revered it as a sacred orientation for prayer. Nevertheless, in the West's end is also its beginning; for many early Eurasian societies it was also the direction associated with rebirth and so became the location for mythical lands of bliss and ease, the afterlife or Paradise. Atlantis, the Fortunate (or Blessed) Isles, Elysium, the Hesperides, Hy Brasil, Avalon, St Brendan's Island: these are just some of the places – mainly islands – that were believed to lie somewhere in the west. They inspired J. R. R. Tolkien in his trilogy *The Lord of the Rings*, where Frodo and his companions travel westwards in search of the mystical Undying Lands, a place of redemption and transcendence (in direct opposition to the Dark Lord Sauron, who is constantly associated with the east and south). Like all the other directions, at different times and places the west could mean its exact opposite: a place of death and rebirth; of endings and new beginnings; and a set of contradictory values – liberty, freedom and prosperity; lawlessness, loneliness and consumerism.

The West's remarkably fluid, even protean nature can be visualized by looking at any modern world map. There is no continuous geographical place called 'the West'. Like all the other cardinal directions, it simply does not exist as a universally accepted location. So how has the West taken on such a defining political identity, and has it triumphed? Or is it, as the early twentieth-century polymath Oswald Spengler believed, in inexorable decline? The term is now so pervasive that in 1985 the historian John Roberts could publish a book entitled *The Triumph of the West*, in which he claimed that 'the story of western civilisation is now the story of mankind, its influence so diffused that old oppositions and antitheses are now meaningless'.[2] The teleological presumptions of Roberts' argument have since been challenged and revised, but the notion of the 'West' as a concrete reality has become firmly fixed in the global imagination, whether as a 'westerner' you live within and endorse it or you live outside and criticize it.

The paradox of the west is that for many societies it represented mortality and oblivion but also the possibility of resurrection and new horizons. As a result, it is never a direction for religious supplication or intercession. In many languages it has directly negative connotations. In ancient Mayan culture the west (*chikin*) was associated with black, and houses were rarely oriented facing westwards. In Central America this was perhaps a practical response to avoiding the afternoon heat, but it also symbolized a turning away from the west as a place of death and blackness.[3] East African communities made similar connections. The Tugen people of Kenya call the west *cherongo*, which is also associated with mortality, darkness and infertility, in direct contrast to its eastern axis, called *kong Asis*, which is closely related to life, light and fecundity.[4]

Yet the emergence of beliefs in reincarnation led many other cultures to see the possibility of new beginnings, even new worlds, in the west. One of the earliest manifestations of this apparent contradiction can be found in the beliefs of ancient Egypt. The west – *imnt*, or 'right' – was the region of both death and rebirth, represented in the roles of the deities Aset (or Isis, the 'Great Mother') and Amentet, goddess of death. Amentet – whose literal translation is 'She of the West' – was believed to originate in Libya (to the west of Egypt). Her name was synonymous with the west bank of the Nile and the world of the dead. As goddess of the underworld, Isis helped the dead – often referred to as 'westerners' – reach the afterlife and was present when her brother and husband Osiris judged them. Aset was also often represented as Amentet, whose headdress contained the hieroglyph 'Emblem of the West', usually depicted as an ostrich feather. The western associations of Aset and Amentet show its paradoxical connotations: from the spiritual journey towards inevitable death in the west emerges the promise of rebirth and new life.[5]

Classical Greek thinkers and writers took up the Egyptian idea of the sacred west at the end of both life and the world, imagining it as a more bucolic place of bliss and ease. With no geographical understanding of a separate continent to the west of Europe and Africa, they located various islands there, floating somewhere in the Atlantic, populated by nothing apart from the hopes and fears of their creators. The earliest Greek texts called it Elysium – from the Greek for 'joy' and 'pure' – the home of the blessed and heroic after death. In Homer's *Odyssey*, it is described as the Elysian 'plain' or 'field', at 'the end of the world'. Here 'life glides on in immortal ease', with 'no snow, no winter onslaught, never a downpour' of rain. It is where Oceanus 'sends up breezes', with 'the singing winds of the West refreshing all mankind'.[6] Oceanus here stood for the Greek Titan and son of Gaia (personifying the Earth) and Uranus (personifying the sky). Oceanus also represents the encircling ocean that the Greeks believed surrounded the Earth's land mass.

Hesiod (fl. 700 BCE) gave the idea greater geographical definition in his *Theogony* and *Works and Days*. Like Homer he reserved this western world as a place for those favoured by the gods, but he too transformed it into an island. In *Works and Days* he claimed that Zeus granted some survivors of the Trojan War 'a life and home apart from men, and settled them at the ends of the Earth. These dwell with carefree heart in the Isles of the Blessed Ones, beside deep-swirling Oceanus.'[7] These 'Blessed' (or sometimes known as the 'Fortunate') islands were also the home of the Hesperides, the 'Daughters of the West' (or 'the Night'), variously described as offspring of Erebus and Night and in some sources the daughters of Atlas. In Hesiod's *Theogony*, the Hesperides were guardians of the 'fair golden apples beyond the famed Oceanus', a wedding present from Gaia to Hera, wife of Zeus.[8]

In the twelve labours of Heracles the eleventh task required stealing the golden apples guarded by the Hesperides in the far west. This is where Heracles discovers the Titan Atlas, condemned to hold up the heavens for ever after rebelling against the gods. Heracles tricks Atlas into taking the apples from the Hesperides while Heracles holds up the sky for him. But then he deceives the unfortunate Titan into assuming his burden yet again, while he runs off with the apples. During his twelve labours our hero created the so-called 'Pillars of Heracles', the promontories or 'pillars' in the Strait of Gibraltar that marked the westernmost point in Greek classical geography. To the west lay the Atlantic – named after Atlas and an extension of the mountain range in Morocco.

Somewhere in this sea, Plato, writing in his *Timaeus* and *Critias*, placed the island of Atlantis. He describes it as 'an island larger than Libya [or Africa] and Asia combined' that was suddenly destroyed by an earthquake. The obsessive pursuit of this 'lost' island that has consumed so many over the centuries misses Plato's point: for him Atlantis is an insular allegory that stands in contrast to Athens and debates about the ideal political state. Its exact geographical location is a chimera, but the inspiration to locate it in the west is not. Moving across land is one thing; to cross water by sailing beyond the horizon inspires more inchoate feelings of fear and loss. The Greeks could and did travel eastwards across the lands of Persia and onwards to India. But moving westwards was limited by the boundary of the Pillars of Heracles and soon ran into an empty, mysterious and unknown ocean, the vast, 'dark sea' of the Atlantic. Like Elysium, Atlantis existed just beyond the limits of the known Greek experience, where myth and reality collided. Both were ideal spaces of death and repose; apparently real yet obviously imagined, of this world but also beyond it.

Fifth-century Gaelic folklore described a different kind of island of eternal bliss lying off the west coast of Ireland, called *Ui Breasail* or *Hy Brasil* (from the Old Irish 'beauty' and 'mighty').[9] Fog obscured the island, which was said to be visible for only one day in every seven years. The tradition of describing such places and their discovery came out of a fusion of Celtic and Christian cultures that led to a specific genre of Irish seafaring adventures called 'immrama', literally 'rowings about'. One of the most famous versions of such a place comes from the Irish monastic saint Brendan of Clonfert (*c.* 484–*c.* 577 CE) and his legendary voyages into the western Atlantic. These were recounted in later tenth-century manuscripts entitled the *Voyage of St Brendan*, following his journey to the west of Ireland in search of paradise. Brendan's seaborne pilgrimage is described in many of these manuscripts as sailing 'westwards to the island which God called the Promised Land of the Saints which God will give to those who come after us at the end of time'.[10] The island was a conflation of the Blessed or Fortunate Isles, Hy Brasil and, somewhat inevitably, St Brendan's Island. The accounts of Brendan's voyage there are often fantastical, involving encounters with Hell, Judas and various devils in pursuit of salvation, appropriating the classical idea of the Blessed Isles in the interests of the Christian story of redemption. The west enabled such wonders because it lacked many of the topographical assumptions and historical associations of the three other cardinal directions. It contained no magnetic pole nor was it a place from which a story of origins began. Free from such attachments, it became more of an imaginative threshold than a geographical place.

For the Irish, as with the Greeks, the west offered a licence to imagine the time after death. The Romans, while inheriting the idea of the Blessed Islands from the Greeks, took a more imperial and geopolitical approach to the idea of the west. In *The Aeneid* (29–19 BCE) the Roman poet Virgil imagined the foundation of Rome as a westward movement across the Mediterranean. The Trojan warrior Aeneas fled the fall of Troy and sailed west to the Italian peninsula in pursuit of his imperial destiny and the birth of the Roman kingdom: what could be called the 'westering' of empire. For the Romans, to travel west represented new possibilities for imperial expansion and cultivation. The trope became known in the Middle Ages as *translatio imperii*, or 'transfer of rule', in which imperial rule is transferred from one empire to another. Often seen as an inexorable move westwards from Persia to Greece, through Rome to 'Western' Christendom, this 'transfer of rule' was central to the idea of *plantation*, the establishment of colonial settlements through 'planting' the seeds of European people and ideas.

The historian Plutarch described the 'Elysian Fields' as islands that were very real and worth cultivating, with the soil 'rich for ploughing and planting . . . sufficient to feed the inhabitants, who may here enjoy all things without trouble or labour'.[11] The Roman idea of the west as a threshold to new worlds and their dominion also brought with it striking prophecies of future discoveries. In Seneca's *Medea* (*c.* 50 CE) the Chorus announces:

> All bounds have been removed, cities have set their walls in new lands, and the world, now passable throughout, has left nothing where it once had place . . . There will come an age in the far-off years when Ocean shall unloose the bonds of things, when the whole broad Earth shall be revealed, when Tethys [Titan goddess and wife of Oceanus] shall disclose new worlds and Thule not be the limit of the lands.[12]

At one level Seneca anticipates the discovery of a 'New World' to the west of Europe: following Columbus's landfall in the Americas in 1492, some Renaissance scholars saw it as a fulfilment of Seneca's lines and the inevitability of the westward *translatio imperii*. But there is also a pessimism in Seneca's account of the breaching of cultural boundaries and loss of a fixed sense of place, generated in part by a very specific historical context: the repressive and volatile political world of imperial Rome under the emperor Nero (37–68 CE). It is another example of the enduring ambiguity of the west as offering hope yet simultaneously threatening loss through the passage of time.

In turning its back on classical polytheistic beliefs, Christianity staked out a clear opposition to the west as the location of Elysium and other Greco-Roman versions of the afterlife. Instead, the Garden of Eden was located in direct contrast firmly in the east. Basic orientation based on Jewish traditions also provided the west with a negative dimension: in Hebrew, 'west' and 'behind' stands in contrast to 'east', 'in front'. Within the Christian Latin tradition such negative associations further intensified. Isidore of Seville argued that the 'west (*occidens*) is named because it makes the day set (*occidere*), and perish, for it hides the light from the world and brings on darkness.'[13]

In keeping with the idea of the west as a gateway rather than a place, Christian writers developed an idea about the geography of the west and divine providence that unified time and space. The twelfth-century theologian Hugh of St Victor's vision of the Earth as an ark also contained an eschatological belief that the end of the world and resurrection would come from the west. As 'time proceeded towards its end, the centre of events would have shifted to the west, so that we may recognize out of this that the world nears its end in time as the course of events has already reached the extremity of the world in space.'[14] Once the location of the afterlife was removed from the terrestrial world, Christianity could reinvest in the idea of the discovery of the west as anticipating the Day of Judgement, the Second Coming of Christ and the Messianic Age. Such a belief in simultaneous destruction and renewal would influence most subsequent religious and secular understandings of the west.

Western Approaches

Columbus famously refused to accept he had encountered a separate western continent *en route* to the east. However, his first voyage to the Americas in 1492 was the beginning of a transformation in Christian European theories of the west and it inspired one of the few world maps oriented with west at the top. In 1500 his chief pilot and navigator, the Spanish Juan de la Cosa, drew the earliest known world chart to show Columbus's landfall (Plate 21). It is an object caught between two worlds, looking both east and west. As a sea chart it draws on the tradition of portolans and is covered with 32-point compass roses and navigational rhumb lines. Yet it also looks like earlier *mappae-mundi*, with its rich decoration and fantastical kingdoms depicted in Asia and Africa. The chart is made from two pieces of vellum (calf skin) stitched together, one covering Africa and Asia, the other western Europe, the Atlantic and the 'New World' of the emerging Americas. The differing scale of both parts betrays the impact of Columbus's voyages: the curved green land mass embracing Cuba is drawn on a much larger scale than Europe, Africa and Asia. A new world is beginning to emerge to the west: but which way up is the chart?

Traditionally the de la Cosa map is reproduced with north at the top and the west to the left. But the shape of the vellum and the toponymy show it should actually be oriented with west at the top. Usually the outline of the calf's shoulders and neck come at the top of the map, as is the case with the *mappamundi* in Hereford Cathedral. To read most of the legends the right way up, including Africa, Asia and the Atlantic, labelled 'Mare Oceanum', the chart must be oriented westwards. When this is done, the image at the top becomes even more compelling. Above – or to the west – of Cuba is a depiction of St Christopher carrying the infant Jesus across a river. The association with Columbus is striking: like his namesake, the patron saint of travellers, he voyages across the sea, spreading the word of Christ to new-found lands and peoples. The ambiguous position of St Christopher also allows anyone looking at the chart to speculate as to whether Columbus has reached a new land mass to the west or is still heading in the same direction, in pursuit of the east. The chart's religious dimension is reiterated in the largest compass rose in the middle of the Atlantic. At its centre is a depiction of the Holy Family. Orientation and direction are determined by a providential Christian view of history moving westwards from the Old World to the threshold of the New World.

European encounters with indigenous communities in the Americas strengthened the belief that only in the west would they find a manifest destiny of riches, redemption and rebirth. From the mid-sixteenth century the Spanish became convinced of the existence of 'El Dorado', a golden city, empire or ruler located to the west somewhere deep in the South American interior. In 1595 Sir Walter Raleigh went in search of El Dorado in the first of two ill-fated expeditions, failing to find the fabled city, but still believing it lay somewhere just over the western horizon. The cosmological beliefs of the local communities encountered by the Spanish and Raleigh seemed to confirm the power of the west as a place of renewal and rebirth. The Guarayu people of Bolivia told the Jesuits that 'soon after burial, the soul starts a long dangerous journey to the land of Tamoi, which is located in the west', where it is cleansed and given new life.[15] Another Bolivian tribe, the Yuracaré, told the Europeans how their creator, Tiri, decided to retire to the end of the world. 'In order to know its extent, he sent a bird to the four directions of the horizon. On the fourth trip, from the west, the bird returned with beautiful plumage. Tiri went to the west, where he lives with his people who, upon reaching old age, rejuvenate.'[16]

West Meets East

As first the Spanish then the English cast their gazes westward, something similar was happening in Ming China. But for the Chinese, geography obliged them to orient themselves to the unknown in different directions. Situated on the eastern rather than western rim of the vast continent of Eurasia, the Chinese also looked out onto an ocean beyond their shores where magical isles and immortal beings were to be found. The difference was that they looked east for their oceanic wonders. In contrast it was from the west and the north that danger arose: Huns, Turks, Tibetans, Mongols, Uyghurs and all the other nomadic societies living in the often hostile environment of the Eurasian steppe.

Within a larger international context, everything else that

lay to the west of China was known as the 'Western Regions'. This included India, which the Chinese knew as *Tianzhu* (a rendering of 'Hindu'), the first character of which, appropriately, is 'Heaven'. This was where the greatest incarnation of Heaven's spiritual power, Sakyamuni Buddha, is believed to have arisen. It was also the land from which the greatest Indian Buddhist missionaries had come to China. The isles of the immortals to which emperors might dream of sailing lay in the ocean to the east, but heaven lay beyond the Himalayas to the west, over which the Queen Mother of the West presided and to which she welcomed the souls of the faithful. According to Daoist lore, west was also the direction in which its spiritual founder Lao Zi was last seen heading at the end of his life.

When European Jesuit missionaries first started arriving in China in the late sixteenth century, they sought to capitalize on this idea of the west as a Buddhist realm by presenting themselves to the Ming authorities as similarly coming from the west (which of course they did). The strategy quickly proved troublesome, as it persuaded the Chinese that Christians were simply another school of Buddhists. Their mistaken identity got the Jesuits in the door, but burdened them with having to explain why Christianity was not Buddhism and why Jesus was not a Buddha. Rather than abandon the basic fact of their origin, the leading Jesuit of the China mission, Matteo Ricci (1552–1610), attempted to reorganize the Chinese conception of the west. His solution was to propose two versions of the west. The 'Lesser West' contained India and the Indian Ocean, from where the Buddhists had come. Further to the west lay the 'Great West', the land where Jesus had lived and from where the Jesuits now came.

To make his point and explain China's spatial relationships to the greater world, Ricci created in 1602 one of the greatest maps of the era: the *Kunyu wanguo quantu* ('Map of the Ten Thousand

Countries of the Earth'; Plate 22). It adapted European maps in depicting twin western and eastern hemispheres to suit its Chinese context. Oriented with north at the top in line with both European and Chinese beliefs, Ricci's map placed the Pacific rather than the Atlantic at its centre. To the left of China was the Lesser West, including India, and then further to the left, the Greater West including Christian Europe.[17]

The west became so important to Ricci's construction of his identity that he adopted the Chinese nickname *Taixi*, the 'gentleman from the Greater West'. Sometimes he signed himself as 'the European', on others as 'the man from the country of Greater West'. Europe meant nothing to most Chinese, so the latter was the preferable term which could be understood by them. For Ricci, 'there are principles common to both East and West', which implied that the Chinese need not address any fundamental cultural or moral barrier blocking their conversion to Christianity. The path to what the west had to offer was open. As no Chinese had yet travelled to Europe, Ricci was offering the west to his Chinese friends as a promised land where they could realize their hopes for a better – albeit Christian – world.[18]

Time for a New Eden

Even as Matteo Ricci was establishing the Jesuit missions in China, on the other side of the globe, Protestant groups in England were starting to look westwards for the fulfilment of their theological destiny. In 1584 Richard Hakluyt, an ordained priest and political advocate for Tudor and Stuart colonization in the Americas, published his 'Discourse of Western Planting', setting out the benefits to the Elizabethan state and its private investors of establishing colonial plantations in modern-day Virginia.

Hakluyt claimed the west for England's Protestant God and its merchants. 'Having by God's good guiding and merciful direction achieved happily this recent western discovery,' he wrote, 'after the seeking the advancement of the kingdom of Christ, the second chief and principal end of the same is traffic.'[19]

Samuel Purchas, Hakluyt's follower and protégé, went even further in celebrating the Stuart claims to the New World, in *Hakluytus Posthumus, or Purchas his Pilgrimes*, his collection of English travel writing and continuation of Hakluyt's work, published in 1625. Purchas's book was as much a justification of the Anglican world view as an account of the English travelling abroad. The one reinforced the other and, for Purchas, paraphrasing Old Testament prophecies (Malachi 4:2), the English nation could fulfil its religious destiny by travelling westwards to deliver its providential message: 'thus hath God given opportunity by navigation into all parts, that in the sunset and evening of the world, the Sun of righteousness might arise out of our west to illuminate the east, and fill both hemispheres with his brightness'.[20] This brightness would not illuminate Paradise but instead prefigure the Apocalypse and the Day of Judgement. Purchas's logic was indebted to earlier medieval beliefs about the west, such as Hugh of St Victor, given a Protestant imperial spin. Just as the world began in the east at sunrise, so it would end with the sunset in the west, signalling the end of all worldly empires and the creation of a new heaven on Earth. For Purchas, theology, empire and divine judgement all met in the west, and the possibility of a 'New World' in America, in a Protestant version of *translatio imperii*.

For the early English settlers in New England, imbued with a sense of their destiny, the west finally became a place rather than a threshold. The Massachusetts judge, printer and millenarian Samuel Sewall (1652–1730), best known for adjudicating in the Salem witch trials, was convinced that America was most suited to the creation of a new Christian world because 'it was the beginning of the East and the end of the West'.[21] The world, like these two cardinal directions, had finally come full circle; the time for a new Eden was now here. The English poet and priest George Herbert (1593–1633) had already imagined 'Religion, like a pilgrime, westward bent' towards America in his poem 'The Church Militant' (1633), with a heliotropic image of being drawn to the direction of the Sun in the fulfilment of divine destiny:

But as the Sunne still goes both west and east;
So also did the Church by going west
Still eastward go; because it drew more neare
To time and place, where judgement shall appeare.[22]

Such images soon crossed the Atlantic and were taken up by the American revivalist theologian Jonathan Edwards (1703–58). Edwards believed that the Second Coming in the west would even transform cosmology: 'when the sun of righteousness, the sun of the new heavens and new Earth, comes to rise ... the sun shall rise in the west, contrary to the course of this world, or the course of things in the old heavens and Earth.'[23]

The most influential exponent of this transfer of religion and empire to the west was the Irish philosopher and Anglican bishop George Berkeley (1685–1753). Convinced that European culture was depraved and exhausted, Berkeley proposed to establish a college of learning in the Bermudas and spent three years there between 1725 and 1728, before abandoning the plan due to lack of funds. In 1726 he wrote *Verses on the Prospect of Planting Arts and Learning in America*. It began with verses entitled 'America, or the Muse's Refuge, A Prophecy', describing Europe's decay. This was in sharp contrast to the imperial possibilities of America:

Westward the course of empire takes its way;
The first four Acts already past,
A fifth shall close the Drama with the day;
Time's noblest offspring is the last.

Berkeley combined millenarianism with heliocentrism to prophesy that empire, not paradise, would determine America's destiny: as the day of world history moved westwards from sunrise and drew to a close with the setting Sun of its fifth act, the imperial denouement would be played out in the west.[24]

The Wild West

Berkeley's sentiments became part of the template for post-independence America's 'manifest destiny': the belief in the divine right of American settlers to pursue a policy of expansion and settlement towards the Pacific seaboard – at the expense of any indigenous societies that got in the way. The west was a tempting prize and excited such a high degree of land seizure and speculation that George III issued a proclamation in 1763 banning further westward incursions into indigenous territories, phrased in the proclamation as 'any Lands beyond the Heads or Sources of any of the Rivers which fall into the Atlantic Ocean from the West and North West'. These lands, the king declared, 'are reserved to the said Indians'.[25] The colonists disagreed. Closing the west to further settlement set off the first wave of discontentment that would lead to the American Revolution. The west belonged to the Americans, and they were determined to have it. The lust for westward expansion only grew, reaching its zenith a century later.

In 1861 the German-American artist Emanuel Leutze (1816–68) was commissioned to decorate the western staircase of the House of Representatives in the Capitol Building in Washington,

DC, with a six- by nine-metre painted mural (Plate 23). Drawing on Berkeley's poem, *Westward the Course of Empire Takes its Way* depicts a train of pioneer settlers – including one sole black figure – cresting over mountainous terrain in their push westwards. Atop a rocky outcrop in the middle of the painting is an explorer who waves his hat and prepares to raise the US flag in anticipation of reaching the promised western lands of Oregon and California. Several figures point towards America's 'Manifest Destiny' in the west, in contrast to the dark icy terrain they have left behind in the east. The predella at the foot of the mural shows the settlers' final destination: the westernmost point of the Golden Gate strait connecting San Francisco Bay with the Pacific Ocean.[26]

Leutze's mural is an epic symbolic map moving from right to left along an east–west axis, the settlers' trek mimicking the *translatio imperii*. Their faces and destinies are bathed in the golden light of the setting Sun in pursuit of what Leutze called in his notes to the mural's design 'the grand peaceful conquest of the great west'.[27] Leutze was influenced in his design by Hegel and his belief in the westward movement of world history. America, said Hegel, was 'the land of the future, where, in the ages that lie before us, the burden of the World's History shall reveal itself'.[28] America was an exception to Hegel's end of history in Europe because its trajectory lay in the future, beyond historical research.[29] So much of the subsequent time of the American national visual and literary imagination was driven by this Western imperative. Simultaneously it tried to erase any reference to the indigenous communities decimated by exploration and settlement, as well as the history of slavery that had underpinned so many of its achievements – though Leutze seems to have introduced the black figure in the final version of his mural in response to Abraham Lincoln issuing his 'Preliminary Emancipation Proclamation' in September 1862.

The 1860s saw the climax of American dreams of 'Manifest Destiny', from Leutze's mural to the famous slogan 'Go west, young man'. The origins of both phrases are usually attributed to the newspaper editor and sometime politician Horace Greeley (1811–72) in an article he wrote in 1865.[30] Greeley was a passionate advocate for the settlement and colonization of western lands and believed that the agricultural development of the American West could resolve many of the urban problems facing the country's eastern seaboard cities. For the American historian Frederick Jackson Turner, this movement westwards was central to the American character and its 'frontier' mentality. In his enormously influential essay, 'The Significance of the Frontier in American History' (1893), Turner called the frontier 'the meeting point between savagery and civilization'. Extolling the virtues of American 'civilization', he argued that the country's unique

> social development has been continually beginning over again on the frontier. This perennial rebirth, this fluidity of American life, this expansion westward with its new opportunities, its continuous touch with the simplicity of primitive society, furnish the forces dominating American character. The true point of view in the history of this nation is not the Atlantic coast, it is the great West.[31]

Not everyone subscribed to the ideology of America's western frontier mentality and its 'Manifest Destiny'. In 1851 the poet, essayist and naturalist Henry David Thoreau (1817–62) delivered a lecture entitled 'Walking' (also referred to as 'The Wild'), first published posthumously in 1862. It is rightly celebrated for many reasons: as an attempt to find a language of American national identity independent from the European tradition; to transcend the bellicose rhetoric of Manifest Destiny; and to establish a new philosophy of humanity's relation to nature. As Thoreau expressed it in the essay's famous opening lines, 'I wish to speak a word for Nature, for absolute freedom and wildness, as contrasted with a freedom and culture merely civil, – to regard man as an inhabitant, or a part and parcel of Nature, rather than a member of society.'[32] Thoreau's reorientation is replete with ideas about a decisive shift in cardinal directions driven by what he calls the 'subtile magnetism in Nature' that compels him westwards. What he finds there is not the Manifest Destiny of one group over another but a new understanding of Nature. 'The West of which I speak,' writes Thoreau, 'is but another name for the Wild . . . in Wildness is the preservation of the World.'[33] For Thoreau the wild is an independent place – found in America's west – that if respected might enable the emergence of a time for a more open and inclusive humanity.[34]

Thoreau's philosophy stems from the simple act of going 'out of the house for a walk' and being led by what he describes as a symbolic inner compass:

> My needle is slow to settle, varies a few degrees, and does not always point due south-west, it is true, and it has good authority for this variation, but it always settles between west and south-southwest. The future lies that way to me, and the Earth seems more unexhausted and richer on that side.

His needle turns him away from the east. 'Eastward I go only by force; but westward I go free. Thither no business leads me. It is hard for me to believe that I shall find fair landscapes or sufficient wildness and freedom behind the eastern horizon.' Thoreau inverts the tradition of regarding east as synonymous with 'front' and west with 'back' by literally turning his back on Europe and instead facing and walking towards the west. 'I must walk toward Oregon,' he writes, 'and not toward Europe. And that way the nation is moving, and I may say that mankind progress from east to west.'[35]

Thoreau appreciated the longer European perception of the west, rhapsodizing that:

Every sunset which I witness inspires me with the desire to go to a West as distant and as fair as that into which the sun goes down ... The island of Atlantis, and the islands and gardens of the Hesperides, a sort of terrestrial paradise, appear to have been the Great West of the ancients, enveloped in mystery and poetry. Who has not seen in imagination, when looking into the sunset sky, the gardens of the Hesperides, and the foundation of all those fables?[36]

In acknowledging these 'fables', Thoreau also wanted to create a new national story that was only just beginning, rather than coming to an end. The switch from the Old World of the classics and Europe in the east to the New World of enterprise and wealth is captured in his neat observation: '[t]o use an obsolete Latin word, I might say, *Ex Oriente lux; ex Occidente FRUX*. From the East light; from the West fruit.'[37] He goes on to sketch an American destiny in stark contrast to that of the long European perception of the west. It would set the tone for much of America's subsequent imaginative time and geography and sense of its place in the world:

We go eastward to realize history and study the works of art and literature, retracing the steps of the race; we go westward as into the future, with a spirit of enterprise and adventure. The Atlantic is a Lethean stream, in our passage over which we have had an opportunity to forget the Old World and its institutions. If we do not succeed this time, there is perhaps one more chance for the race left before it arrives on the banks of the Styx; and that is in the Lethe of the Pacific, which is three times as wide.[38]

Thoreau's poetic vision of the west as a pioneering frontier of endless reinvention and opportunity challenged the more aggressive American settler mentality of Manifest Destiny. Its expansiveness also placed the west on a spectrum that enabled later writers to imagine wildly different versions of it. The journalist and poet Arthur Chapman (1873–1935) wrote his poem 'Out Where the West Begins' (1917) in response to press debates as to where the west actually began on a map of the United States. Chapman's poem was part of a new genre of 'cowboy poetry'. Endlessly anthologized and parodied, the poem drew on standard ideas of the west, from its topographical vividness to its overwhelmingly masculine outlook:

> Out where the handclasp's a little stronger,
> Out where the smile dwells a little longer,
> That's where the West begins;
> Out where the sun is a little brighter,
> Where the snows that fall are a trifle whiter,
> Where the bonds of home are a wee bit tighter,
> That's where the West begins.

In Chapman's poem the western skies are bluer and the men truer than in all other directions. It is where the 'world is in the making', even though the poem made no attempt to settle the geographical dispute as to in which state the west began. Chapman echoed Thoreau's vision, a perception of enterprising Americans moving ever westwards that anticipated the development of US foreign policy from one of non-intervention in the mid-nineteenth century to a geopolitical position of global dominance by the later twentieth century.

How the West was Won

This was also the period in which our modern idea of the West was properly established in the English-speaking world, as the western part of the world.[39] The powerful yet contradictory beliefs about the west that had existed since ancient times mutated into one overriding modern political idea. More than any other cardinal direction – including east – west became detached from its origins as a direction and transformed into an ideology. Today, 'the West' is broadly understood as a culture and civilization originating first in Europe then in North America, set in opposition to the societies and religions of Asia and Africa.

Even as the West emerged as a geopolitical thought in the nineteenth century, writers and intellectuals from outside Europe and North America were using it to explain what their societies lacked. The Japanese writer and journalist Fukuzawa Yukichi (1835–1901) was one of the most eloquent voices in favour of westernization and part of a reforming movement during the Meiji period (1868–1912). Having visited Europe and North America from the 1850s, he published an enthusiastic essay on 'Conditions in the West' (1866) which argued that Japan must modernize according to Western principles. In his highly influential book *An Outline of a Theory of Civilization* (1875), Fukuzawa insisted that the starting point for reforming Japan's institutions 'lies in sweeping away blind attachment to past customs and adopting the spirit of Western civilization'.[40]

From where Fukuzawa stood, this 'West' did lie to the west of Japan at the far western end of the Eurasian continent. But Japan felt its presence reaching more powerfully from the east across the Pacific. Even though the West lay east, the trope of the West as the advanced zone of the globe so convinced the Japanese that they accepted the position it assigned them: the Far East. The irony was not lost on Fukuzawa that Japan needed to break away from the Asian East (which lay to its west) and declare itself a candidate for Western status. He made the point in an editorial in 1885 under the stirring title, 'Datsu-A ron', which could be translated as 'Good-bye Asia' but really means 'Leaving Asia behind'. He called for Japan to modernize and effectively become a western outlier in Asia. 'We do not have time to wait for the enlightenment of our neighbours so that we can work together toward the development of Asia,' he wrote. 'It is better for us to leave the ranks of Asian nations and cast our lot with civilized nations of the West.'[41] His editorial foregrounded Japan's embrace of industrialization, technology and military power that placed it, at least economically, within the ambit of the West.

Ziya Gökalp (1876–1924), the Turkish nationalist and voice of modern 'Turkism', also took inspiration from Japan and Fukuzawa. In his support for Turkish republicanism prior to the collapse of the Ottoman Empire in 1922, Gökalp advocated a westwards development of Turkishness. The classic Ottoman state modelled itself on what Gökalp called 'the civilization of the Far East'. With the collapse of the empire and their 'transition to the stage of the nation-state', the Turks seemed 'determined to accept Western civilization'. He put the case for Turkish nationalism bluntly, insisting that 'we have to accept the civilization of the West, because, if we do not we shall be enslaved by the powers of the West'. Gökalp's fusion of Western values, Turkish nationalism and Islam remains hugely powerful – and influential: he is admired by the Islamist Turkish president Recep Tayyip Erdogan, who was imprisoned for four months in 1999 for reciting one of Gökalp's more militant poems. In turning away from the eastern 'Orient' and promising a distinct Turkish identity drawing on both Eastern and Western traditions, Gökalp's influence has only grown as the country continues to be seen by many as legitimizing an increasingly authoritarian and xenophobic state policy.

Fukuzawa and Gökalp both understood the West as no longer a direction but a 'civilization' to be emulated as it spread across the world before the outbreak of the First World War. The Bolshevik Revolution in Russia in 1917 drew an increasingly absolute line between the West as the domain of capitalism and Soviet Russia as its Marxist-Leninist antithesis. The events of 1917 were not initially seen as the 'westernization' of Russia: instead they were regarded in much of Europe as an 'Asiatic' revolution that represented a threat to white, Western supremacy, which consolidated a sense of itself in opposition to this 'eastern' political development. Soviet rhetoric from the 1920s went even further and described the West as the counter-revolutionary location of all forms of social and economic inequality, with Stalin explicitly labelling the Soviet Union as 'anti-western'.

Within the same generation the idea of the West as a 'civilization' was already facing its twilight, described most eloquently by the German historian Oswald Spengler (1880–1936). Between 1918 and 1922 Spengler published *Der Untergang des Abendlandes*, translated into English as *The Decline of the West*. The book captured the pessimism of so much European philosophy in the wake of the slaughter of the First World War and the crisis felt by many German intellectuals following their country's defeat in the conflict.

A more literal translation of the title of Spengler's book shows it has deeper roots in ideas about the West. 'Untergang' is literally 'going under', and 'Abendland' (usually translated as 'West') is 'evening land', evoking the long-standing idea of the setting Sun 'going under' and into the darkness of the West. The book could easily have been translated into English as 'The Sunset of the West'. Spengler argued that the twentieth century saw the fulfilment – or 'decline' – of what he called 'West-European–American' culture.[42] He believed that all great world cultures, from the Babylonian through Chinese, Mesoamerican,

Greco-Roman and Arabian societies, flourished as cultures then hardened into civilizations before facing inevitable decline and demise. 'Looked at this way,' wrote Spengler, 'the "Decline of the West" comprises nothing less than the problem of *Civilization*.' Each civilization was 'a conclusion, the thing-become succeeding the thing-becoming, death following life, rigidity following expansion, intellectual age and the stone-built, petrifying world city following mother-earth . . . They are an end irrevocable yet by inward necessity reached again and again.'[43] For Spengler, time was running out for the West. He argued that the 'soil of the West [was] metaphysically exhausted'. The decline of Western civilization would lead to profound inequality and authoritarian politics, what he called 'the dictature of money' and 'the coming of Caesarism' in a striking prefiguration of the economic turmoil of interwar Europe and the rise of Nazism.[44]

Spengler's gloomy prognostications captured what many of his contemporaries believed, and they continue to exert an influence on conservative and libertarian commentators and policymakers. Those who understood the West as an irresistible political and economic force driven by capitalism, technology and mass democracy also simultaneously began to pronounce its decline, even demise, ranging from books such as James Little's *The Doom of Civilization* (1907) to Douglas Murray's *The War on the West* (2022). Almost as soon as the West acquired its modern definition, its eclipse was announced in an uncanny repetition of the long-standing tradition from the Egyptians to the Tudors of seeing it as the place of both death *and* rebirth.

Others who drew on Spengler included the political scientist Samuel Huntington, and his theory of the 'clash of civilizations' (1993) that shaped so much US foreign policy in the Arabian Gulf and Afghanistan following the attacks on 9/11, and the right-wing American politician Patrick J. Buchanan, in his book *The Death of the West* (2001). Spengler's ideas have even been revisited by American commentators trying to understand the growth of neoliberal and authoritarian impulses in American political life that led to the rise of Donald Trump.[45]

Spengler imagined the life cycle of cultures developing into civilizations, leading to their inevitable decline and decay through 'notions of birth, death, youth, age'. Yet this was not a new story: it went back to the assumptions surrounding the heliocentric movement of the Sun from east to west, sunrise to sunset, that could be traced to ancient Egyptian cosmology and long-standing ideas of *translatio imperii*. The difference is that Spengler's melancholy scenario offered no chance of rebirth, no redemption and no Elysium. Instead, modern Western culture – which he named 'Faustian', after his hero Goethe's Faust – faced the long twilight of a civilization characterized by personal alienation and political authoritarianism.

Spengler's pessimism evolved out of a wider political crisis within European and American culture as the confident assumptions of the nineteenth century collapsed and the world descended into war in 1914. In the decade following its publication the book seemed to anticipate so much that was wrong with the West: the exuberant frenzy of the 'Roaring Twenties' in the United States and Europe, a cycle of economic boom and bust that would lead to the financial crash of 1929 and the rise of extreme political ideologies, including Nazism.

It is little wonder Spengler's arguments resonated with so many intellectuals disillusioned with Europe's Age of Reason or Enlightenment – a word with its own directional associations of brightness and sunrise. With the rise of anti-imperial struggles for independence and decolonization post-1945, those colonized by Western powers took up Spengler's idea of the 'decline of the West' in a process subsequently described as 'the empire writes back'.[46]

In a striking inversion of the Western tradition of Orientalism inventing the idea of the East to dominate and exploit it, politicians and writers from Africa and Asia adopted a strategy of 'Occidentalism'. This involved the stereotyping of modern Western people and their societies as variously materialistic, decadent, faithless and violent latter-day Crusaders.[47] In 1962 the Iranian writer Seyyed Jalāl Āl-e Ahmad (1923–69) published a book translated into English as *Occidentosis: A Plague from the West*. Āl-e Ahmad used the Persian term *Gharbzadegi* – variously translated as 'Westoxification', 'Westitis' and 'Euromania', as well as 'Occidentosis'. As these terms imply, Āl-e Ahmad describes the West as a toxic disease or infestation that 'plagues' societies such as Iran in what many of his contemporaries regarded as one of the most important works in modern Iranian history. For Āl-e Ahmad the West was an infection, draining the East of its resources and collective identity:

> 'East' and 'West' are no longer geographical or political concepts to me. For a European or an American, the West means Europe and America and the East, the USSR, China, and the Eastern European nations. But for me, they are economic concepts. The West comprises the sated nations and the East, the hungry nations.[48]

The West was an economic and psychological poison: less of an identity, more like a virus infecting the globe. Āl-e Ahmad's answer to this malaise was to encourage Iranian self-determination, technological innovation, rapid industrialization and economic independence from the West.

A version of Āl-e Ahmad's 'Occidentosis' – closely connected to the more familiar terms of 'Occidentalism' and 'anti-Westernism' – has shaped much global political language and beliefs since the late twentieth century, voiced by those from the West and outside it. But despite the many anti-imperialist notices echoing Spengler and declaring its imminent demise, the West continues to exert a potent force across the globe, able to draw rich and poor (such as refugees) from the places where they were born into places they have never before experienced. Many Chinese, for example, are still vulnerable to this idea of the West, even if this attitude has been labelled as politically 'incorrect'. The east–west polarity developed under Mao Zedong during the third quarter of the twentieth century celebrated the East as the zone of authentic origin and political purity and the West as the place of corruption and decline, in an echo of the Soviet rhetoric following the Bolshevik Revolution. After the fervour of the Cultural Revolution, for many Chinese the East was no longer the direction to conjure. In the rush for the personal wealth that capitalism promises, the virtue of being in the East has lost some of its appeal. Far better to head West if you can – wherever that is.

The enduring symbol of the West in terms of economics and geopolitics remains the United States, both for its supporters and its critics. In recent decades its relative decline in the face of Asian economic growth has become a truism. This has also led to changes in America's perception of its own West. One of the most innovative recent explorations of this changing nature was described by the American writer Richard Rodriguez in his essay 'True West: Relocating the Horizon of the American Frontier' (1996). Rodriguez – who grew up in California as the gay son of Mexican migrants – pushes back against Thoreau's perspective, with its east–west orientation. 'In the 1950s, California was filling with westering Americans who were confident they had arrived,' writes Rodriguez. 'My parents were from Mexico. My father described California, always, as "*el norte*". My father's description had latitude, allowed for more America. To have grown up with a father who spoke of California as the North, a Chicago-accented neighbour who spoke of California as the West, to have grown up thinking of the West as lying east of here, is already to have noticed that "West" is imaginary.' Rodriguez acknowledges the ambivalent legacy of Thoreau and more strident supporters of America's western frontier: 'American myth has traditionally been written east to west, describing an elect people's manifest destiny . . . of man's license to dominate Nature.' It is a powerful yet exclusive mythology: the 'United States of America is letter-box formatted to exclude Canada and Mexico', both of which Rodriguez sees, in an echo of Hamlin's Canadian 'Nordic Index', as 'north/south countries – neither has a myth of the West'. In contrast, 'America is conceived by Americans longitudinally', from east to west.[49]

Yet, in drawing on his mixed heritage, Rodriguez discerns a shift in America's orientation. 'The United States never had a true North until now,' he claims. 'The American Civil War divided the nation: impressed upon the Union the distinctiveness of the regional South. But the North was never more than a political idea.' Two years before Rodriguez's essay was published, the North American Free Trade Agreement was ratified. 'For the United States,' writes Rodriguez, 'NAFTA represents a revolutionary recalibration to north and south.' NAFTA – a trading axis between Canada, Mexico and the United States, and its successor USMCA (2020), the United States-Mexico-Canada Agreement – signals a significant economic shift from north to south, alongside mass migration that is beginning to reorient America's geographical and political axis. From where Rodriguez stands, 'California is inventing a rectified North', connecting Los Angeles with Vancouver and Seattle, 'the capital of the new North'. Rodriguez feels his 'future more closely aligned to British Columbia than to Massachusetts'. Standing in the Pacific littoral facing east, Rodriguez observes 'how the metaphor of the West dissolves into foam at my feet'.[50]

Just as in the language of international development the East has been assimilated into the 'Global South', so too the American

West is now turning not just to the North, but also to the East. A recent trope in the American West is that 'true west' now lies *east* of California. Disaffected Californians who have come to view the erstwhile Golden State as an unaffordable, congested, environmentally ravaged dystopia are now migrating east to states like Utah, Nevada, Arizona and Texas – in order, as they see it, 'to get back West'. And so these departing Californians – bound eastwards on the map, but westwards in their heads – seek a surrogate dream state, a place that can reconnect them with a frontier ethos that was, from the outset, a fantasy. This seems like a suitably recursive place to leave the West, that most temporal and metaphorical of all cardinal directions. Whether from within or without, the idea of the West has travelled through time and space further than any other cardinal direction. Retaining traces of its associations with the setting of the Sun, it has become a pervasive ideology, more even than a direction or a personal identity.

The Blue Dot

In the early 1990s I lived in East Berlin, a place divided between East and West. I befriended an artist in the bohemian district of Prenzlauer Berg who told me a story that has stayed with me ever since. He recalled how, years before the Berlin Wall fell in 1989, he acquired a map prohibited by the East German authorities because it showed the old, unified city before its division in 1961. He would spend hours poring over the map and memorizing the districts and streets of the other half of a divided city in which he lived but doubted he would ever see with his own eyes. On the night of 9 November 1989, like so many other East Berliners, he went over the Wall. He walked the streets of West Berlin that were so familiar to his mind's eye from years of consulting his old map. He explained how he could move with ease around one half of a city he had never seen thanks to the illicit map he had studied for so many years. What struck me was his story of how he was approached for directions by a West Berliner, lost in the chaotic celebration of the Wall's downfall. By successfully directing someone to a street he'd never seen but knew from his mental map, the artist understood that he was no longer an 'Ossie' – the slang for an East German – and had become a generic Berliner.

One of the motivations for writing this book was that I've experienced many similar versions of this story throughout my life. Although a northerner, I've lived mostly in the south of England. As well as my time in East Berlin I've also spent significant periods in South Africa, another country named and demarcated by political powers – in this case European colonial ones – along a north–south rather than east–west axis. And I am also of course identified as a Westerner. North, south, east and west: each direction has at some point defined who I am.

We are all shaped to some degree by the cardinal directions. Our locations and identities only make sense relative to other places and people. The directions offer ways to relate to what surrounds us, in a real as well as a metaphorical sense. They permit us to rise above the maze of our lives, both geographically and spiritually, to assess the direction in which we are going. Yet in today's digital age a grasp of the cardinal directions appears to be waning, and its history can be identified with some precision. On 8 February 2005 Google Maps was launched, claiming that it would help users 'get from A to B'. Less than two years later, on 8 January 2007, Apple announced its first iPhone, a smartphone using multi-touch technology including a map application that Apple CEO Steve Jobs used to demonstrate the phone's capabilities. The following year, in June 2008, the iPhone 3G was released, using the third generation of network technology so phones could connect to the internet wherever the device was located. This enabled Apple to introduce a blue dot on the phone's map application that allowed the user to see and navigate through their current 'live' location, using a combination of global positioning systems (GPS), internet protocol (IP), location and phone-mast triangulation. This combination of online maps and smartphone technology created a virtual revolution. As a consequence, cardinal directions no longer seem to hold the power they exerted in the past. Instead, online users now place themselves at the centre of the map, closely observing not the physical world, but the blue dot that constitutes their surrogate selves in motion.

Some neuroscientists believe that, as a result of surrendering our ability to navigate the space around us to electronic devices, we could also be reducing our mental faculties, or at least that part of the brain which appears to drive spatial cognition. They have identified so-called 'place cells', neurons in and around the hippocampus, the seahorse-shaped part of the brain located deep in the temporal lobe that is responsible for learning and memory. Place cells are activated in certain locations, while more recently discovered 'head-direction cells' respond to which way we face, 'grid cells' respond to position and 'boundary cells' fire up when we confront environmental boundaries. Together these neurons create and store cognitive maps that enable us to remember and retrace our routes and travels over time.[1]

Recent research measured the size of the hippocampus of London taxi drivers required to undertake 'The Knowledge', a test that involves them memorizing the streets, landmarks and quickest routes in the six square miles of central London. In training for the test, it appears that a taxi driver's hippocampus grew, before returning to its normal size after they quit or retired.[2] If the hippocampus can grow because of intensive practical navigation, could it also atrophy over time if we surrender its cognitive functions to online GPS devices? We now seem to be experiencing the apparent waning of the power and function of the four cardinal directions as route-finding devices. The companies providing their online replacements like to boast that we are the last generation that will remember what it means to get lost: but they are reluctant to acknowledge that this could prove to be more of an evolutionary loss than a gain.

Perhaps such fears are misplaced. After all, the earliest uses of the four cardinal directions were as elementary global positioning systems designed to enable archaic societies to situate themselves within their cosmologies and navigate across terrestrial space. They are human symbols derived from a basic grasp of geomagnetism (north–south) and the movement of the Sun (east–west). They have helped individuals navigate, understand and even dominate the natural world. Over time they have evolved to give meaning to the ways societies organize themselves: their contested language and loaded meanings have now become almost purely ideological – northerners versus southerners, the Western world opposing Eastern or 'oriental' societies, the Global South challenging the developed North. This language of geopolitical oppositions, between the North and South, or East and West, and its many intercardinal dimensions is now untethered from any geographical reality. It no longer matters where a country is situated on a map to be labelled according to one direction or another. What counts are the political values they express: Western civilization, Eastern barbarism, the underdeveloped South and so on. The identities they confer – as northerners, southerners, westerners, even easterners – should be treated with caution as pride in that identity can also generate insular parochialism and xenophobia. Reducing places to coordinates also comes at a cost, as in the case of the political geography of a city like East Berlin, but also the climactic depredations in areas such as Antarctica. In our current environmental crisis, places need to be respected in and for themselves and not for their geopolitical meanings or natural resources.

Nevertheless, there is still a need for us to navigate our way through the contemporary world, online and offline, and for devices to point us in the 'right' direction. What is being lost in the digital process is the centrality of the magnetic compass as a prime tool for wayfinding. Online mapping applications are developing methods of automated spatial cognition that supersede the use of compasses. Those like Google Maps are now introducing 'visual positioning' software that allows a device to 'localize' surroundings on a virtual map. This means the application can match a vast store of digital imagery of an urban environment with your smartphone's camera, rather than its inbuilt compass. It delivers more precise directions and provides a clearer understanding of orientation when moving from one location to another, such as stepping out of a subway or a hotel. We are now being guided by digitized photographic data rather than a magnetized needle.

If we have lost what it means to get lost, could our 24/7 digital directions risk disorienting us in a more existential sense? The old sacred and political centres that used to dictate our prime cardinal directions no longer anchor us. Instead, they have given way to a plethora of virtual and local places. For many of us our most important address is our email, accessible wherever we are, regardless of geographical location. Many other physical locations that used to direct our lives – such as supermarkets, banks, law courts, even places for childhood play – are moving online, enabling us to create online *personae* and avatars, symbolized by the blue dot moving through cyberspace. Governments are now adopting policies called 'untact' (as opposed to 'contact') to minimize human interaction in favour of contactless services that increase economic productivity. In such virtual social spaces there seems little interest in or need for the cardinal directions. Their power now resides in their geopolitical connotations, which have eclipsed their directional significance.

Rather than understanding the world based on a two-dimensional, four-sided map with poles running north to south and the arc of the Sun from east to west, we are entering a world of global *multipolarity*, where various political meanings fill the cardinal directions. All four of them are the result of culture and the rules of language; their geopolitical meanings have now eclipsed their use as wayfinding tools. As the polar ice caps melt and the places named north and south seem to shift and dissolve, definitions of east and west also move and switch according to military conflicts and economic upheaval, as seen in the rhetoric surrounding the wars in Ukraine and Gaza and the Global South's attempts to reach 'up' to emulate (or even join) the developed

North, with mass migrations especially between the 'Global North' and the 'Global South'.

In this our digitized century, there are now five directions – north, south, east, west and the online blue dot: 'You'. As paper maps are eclipsed, that dot becomes pre-eminent, superseding compass directions which, for many, become irrelevant. Eyes glued to that jerky little blue ball, we spend less and less travel time observing the physical terrain through which we move, and more time bumping into others as we go. Speed of movement – in cars, trains and aeroplanes – increasingly replaces distance and direction. The compass direction does still linger as a tiny arrow in the bottom corner of our geospatial apps, but most of the time it seems redundant, almost anachronistic. All directions are now localized to wherever you are – usually while checking your mobile device as you move.

That blue dot is now the most extreme expression of a long history of egocentric mapping. The speed and reach of economic globalization leads to the compression of space and distance: what matters most is where we stand and how we consume, often at the expense of an immersive understanding of and interaction with our physical domain. Online mapping has taken us into a new language of what could be called 'technological directionalism'. Directions are of no importance to us as users, but they are for the application, which is designed to ensure that its highly accurate and sophisticated digital plotting is invisible to us, stripping out any of its historical and ideological connotations. There is no longer a concern with the political language games that have characterized the deeper history of the cardinal directions as described in this book. We just want to move as quickly and conveniently as we can, as the cardinal directions wither away. Individuals online can be virtually connected but environmentally detached from the surrounding world, inhabiting a confused realm of spatial illiteracy. As Michael Bond points out in his book *Wayfinding*, 'for the first time in the history of human evolution, we have stopped using many of the spatial skills that have sustained us for tens of thousands of years'. He worries that online mapping devices leave many of us in a situation where, 'in exchange for the absolute certainty of knowing where we are in space, we sacrifice our sense of place'.[3]

In just five decades the world has gone from embracing one blue dot to another. The first was the breathtaking image described at the beginning of this book: the photograph of the whole Earth taken by the astronauts onboard the Apollo 17 mission in December 1972. It showed Earth, a precious azure marble floating in a vast, dark, empty universe. The image reminded all those who saw it of the singular fragility of the beautiful blue world we all inhabit and the need to think beyond ourselves in taking care of it. Yet one technological innovation soon superseded another. The pixellated virtual blue dot that started to appear on our smartphones from 2008 onwards has now displaced the planetary one, transforming our orientation from looking outwards and beyond ourselves to turning inwards with little sense of the wider world through which we move. This subtle shift in scalar contrast risks a dramatic downscaling and reorientation of our shrinking global world.

The four cardinal directions are as much the creation of the human imagination as the Poles, the Equator, the Tropics and any of the prime meridians established by empires over the centuries. As the sunrise – and sunset – recedes from those lives lived in built-up urban environments, we are becoming disoriented from the natural world. Online technology has created a new practice and language where applications do the directional work we are unwilling – or increasingly incapable – of doing. Each direction is now defined for all but technical specialists by geopolitical beliefs and identities rather than direction and navigation. The two blue dots remind us that the cardinal directions which have at different times both oriented and disoriented humans for millennia are themselves subject to reorientation. Now more than ever, each cardinal direction is defined by and even comes to mean its opposite. North and South, East and West are mobile, unstable ideas that change and flip under pressure from the rise and fall of geopolitical forces, technological innovation, cultural beliefs and the language games we play.

What is the next direction in this world of multipolarity and disorientation? The world picture established over the last 500 years, with north at the top and ruled by Western powers, need no longer hold us captive. Politically, our orientation could shift 90 degrees to the east, with China's economic power redefining who and where is on 'top'. Perhaps a future African 'Renaissance' led by the Global South will spin the globe a further 90 degrees and put the birthplace of humanity back at the centre of our world picture. And both circular blue dots remind us that more than ever we live on a mutually interdependent globe. The history of the four cardinal directions poses a question for their future in our digital twenty-first century. A spherical globe has no need for them, so why should we?

Notes

ORIENTATION

1. Al Reinert, 'The Blue Marble Shot: Our First Complete Photograph of Earth', *The Atlantic* (12 April 2011).

2. Ludwig Wittgenstein, *Philosophical Investigations*, ed. and trans. G. E. M. Anscombe, P. M. S. Hacker and Joachim Schulte (Blackwell, Oxford, 2009).

3. See Michael Bond, *Wayfinding: The Art and Science of How We Find and Lose Our Way* (Pan Macmillan, London, 2020), p. 94.

4. Bond, *Wayfinding*, p. 84.

5. David Barrie, *Incredible Journey: Exploring the Wonders of Animal Navigation* (Hodder, London, 2019); Carol Grant Gould and James L. Gould, *Nature's Compass: The Mystery of Animal Navigation* (Princeton University Press, Princeton, 2012).

6. S. Yoshitake, 'Japanese Names for the Four Cardinal Points', *Bulletin of the School of Oriental Studies*, University of London, 7, 1 (1933), pp. 91–103.

7. Amani Lusekelo, 'Terms for Cardinal Directions in Eastern Bantu Languages', *Journal of Humanities* (Zomba), 26 (2018), pp. 49–71: pp. 57–8.

8. Thomas J. Bassett, 'Indigenous Mapmaking in Intertropical Africa', in *The History of Cartography*, vol. 2, bk 3: *Cartography in the Traditional African, American, Arctic, Australian, and Pacific Societies*, ed. David Woodward and G. Malcolm Lewis (Chicago University Press, Chicago, 1998), pp. 24–48: p. 26.

9. Yigal Levin, 'Nimrod the Mighty, King of Kish, King of Sumer and Akkad', *Vetus Testamentum*, 52 (2002), pp. 350–66: p. 360.

10. The following discussion of the clay-tablet map draws on A. R. Millard, 'Cartography in the Ancient Near East', in *The History of Cartography*, vol. 1: *Cartography in Prehistoric, Ancient, and Medieval Europe and the Mediterranean*, ed. J. B. Harley and David Woodward (Chicago

University Press, Chicago, 1987); Ruth Josie Wheat, *Terrestrial Cartography in Ancient Mesopotamia*, PhD thesis, University of Birmingham, 2012; and Nadezhda Freedman, 'The Nuzi Ebla', *The Biblical Archaeologist*, 40, 1 (1977), p. 32. I am extremely grateful to Professor Millard for sharing his expertise on the map in email correspondence.

11. See E. Unger, 'Ancient Babylonian Maps and Plans', *Antiquity*, 9 (1935), pp. 311–22; J. Neumann, 'The Winds in the World of the Ancient Mesopotamian Civilizations', *Bulletin of the American Meteorological Society*, 58, 10 (1977), pp. 1050–55; and Wayne Horowitz, *Mesopotamian Cosmography* (Eisenbrauns, Winona Lake, Indiana, 1998).

12. John B. Haviland, 'Guugu Yimithirr Cardinal Directions', *Ethos*, 26, 1 (1998), pp. 25–47.

13. Cecil H. Brown, 'Where do Cardinal Directions Come From?', *Anthropological Linguistics*, 25, 2 (1983), pp. 121–61.

14. Lusekelo, 'Terms for Cardinal Directions in Eastern Bantu Languages', and Angelika Mietzner and Helma Pasch, 'Expressions of Cardinal Directions in Nilotic and Ubangian Languages', *SKASE Journal of Theoretical Linguistics*, 4, 3 (2007), pp. 1–16.

15. The following description of Mesoamerican cardinal directions draws on Miguel Leon-Portilla, *Aztec Thought and Culture: A Study of the Ancient Nahuatl Mind* (University of Oklahoma Press, Norman, Oklahoma, 1963), pp. 25–61. I am extremely grateful to Dr Caroline Dodds Pennock for sharing her expertise with me on the subject and providing some of these sources.

16. Theophrastus, 'On Winds', in Victor Coutant and Val L. Eichenlaub (eds. and trans.), *Theophrastus: De Ventis* (University of Notre Dame Press, Notre Dame, Indiana, 1975), p. 3, quoted in Barbara Obrist, 'Wind Diagrams and Medieval Cosmology', *Speculum*, 72, 1 (1997), pp. 33–84: p. 38.

17. Quoted in Alessandro Nova, 'The Role of the Winds in Architectural Theory from Vitruvius to Scamozzi', in Barbara Kenda (ed.), *Aeolian Winds and the Spirit in Renaissance Architecture* (Routledge, London, 2006), pp. 70–86: pp. 71–2.

18. See John MacDonald, *The Arctic Sky: Inuit Astronomy, Star Lore, and Legend* (Royal Ontario Museum, Toronto, 1998), pp. 173–82.

19. A. K. Brown, 'The English Compass Points', *Medium Ævum*, 47, 2 (1978), pp. 221–46.

20. G. J. Marcus, 'Hafvilla: A Note on Norse Navigation', *Speculum*, 30, 4 (1955), pp. 601–5.

21. Tatjana N. Jackson, 'On the Old Norse System of Spatial Orientation', *Saga-Book: The Viking Society for Northern Research*, 25 (1998–2001), pp. 72–82.

22. For a general history of magnetism, see Gillian Turner, *North Pole, South Pole: The Epic Quest to Solve the Great Mystery of Earth's Magnetism* (The Experiment, New York, 2010).

23. Petra Schmidl, 'Two Early Arabic Sources on the Magnetic Compass', *Journal of Arabic and Islamic Studies*, 1 (2017), pp. 81–132.

24. Quoted in Thomas Wright (ed.), *Alexandri Neckam, De Naturis Rerum* (London, 1863), p. xxxiv.

25. Quoted in E. G. R. Taylor, *The Haven-Finding Art: A History of Navigation from Odysseus to Captain Cook* (Hollis and Carter, London, 1956), p. 100.

26. Peregrinus, *The Letter of Petrus Peregrinus, 'On the Magnet'*, AD 1269, trans. Brother Arnold (McGraw, New York, 1904), p. 8.

27. Peregrinus, *'On the Magnet'*, pp. 10–11.

28. Peregrinus, *'On the Magnet'*, p. 19.

29. John Seller, a seventeenth-century English publisher and map-maker, quoted in Deborah Warner, 'Terrestrial Magnetism: For the Glory of God and the Benefit of Mankind', *Osiris*, 9 (1994), pp. 66–84: p. 73.

30. Stephen Pumfrey, *Latitude and the Magnetic Earth* (Icon Books, London, 2002).

31. Willim Gilbert, 'Preface' in *On the Magnet*, ed. Derek J. Price, trans. P. F. Mottelay (Dover, New York, 1958), sig. ij. Jim Bennett, 'Cosmology and the Magnetic Philosophy', *Journal of the History of Astronomy*, 12 (1981), pp. 165–77.

32. Quoted in N. H. de Vaudrey Heathcote, 'Christopher Columbus and the Discovery of Magnetic Variation', *Science Progress in the Twentieth Century*, 27, 105 (1932), pp. 82–103: p. 83.

33. Lori L. Murray and David R. Bellhouse, 'How Was Edmond Halley's

Map of Magnetic Declination (1701) Constructed?', *Imago Mundi*, 69, 1 (2017), pp. 72–84.

EAST

1. Quoted in David N. Keightley, *The Ancestral Landscape: Time, Space, and Community in Late Shang China (ca. 1200–1045 BC)* (University of California Press, Berkeley, 2000), p. 27.

2. Qun Rene Chen, 'Cardinal Meanings in Chinese Language: Their Cultural, Social and Symbolic Meanings', *ETC: A Review of General Semantics*, 66, 2 (2009), pp. 225–39.

3. Yoshitake, 'Japanese Names for the Four Cardinal Points', pp. 99–100.

4. Chen, 'Cardinal Meanings', p. 236.

5. Quoted in Paul F. Bradshaw, *Daily Prayer in the Early Church: A Study of the Origin and Development of the Divine Office* (Wipf and Stock, Oregon, 1981), p. 11.

6. Here and all subsequent references are to the King James Bible.

7. James Donaldson et al. (ed.), *The Sacred Writings of Apostolic Teaching and Constitution* (Verlag, Augsburg, 2012), p. 55.

8. Franz Landsberger, 'The Sacred Direction in Synagogue and Church', *Hebrew Union College Annual*, 28 (1957), pp. 181–203: p. 196.

9. https://kupdf.net/download/the-spirit-of-the-liturgy-cardinal-joseph-ratzinger_598c2e1adcod602114300d19_pdf

10. Quoted in Alessandro Scafi, *Mapping Paradise: A History of Heaven on Earth* (British Library, London, 2006), p. 125.

11. Quoted in Jerry Brotton, *A History of the World in Twelve Maps* (Penguin, London, 2012), p. 104.

12. Quoted in Scafi, *Mapping Paradise*, pp. 126–7.

13. Ibid.

14. Quoted in Mustafa Yilmaz and Ibrahim Tiryakioglu, 'The Astronomical Orientation of the Historical Grand Mosques in Anatolia (Turkey)', *Archive for History of Exact Sciences*, 72, 6 (2018), pp. 565–90: p. 567.

15. Quoted and discussed in Yilmaz and Tiryakioglu, 'Astronomical Orientation', pp. 568–9.

16. Bassett, 'Indigenous Mapmaking', pp. 39–40.

17. Sigmund Eisner (ed.), *A Treatise on the Astrolabe by Geoffrey Chaucer* (University of Oklahoma Press, Norman, 2002), p. 120.

18. Suzanne Conklin Akbari, *Idols in the East: European Representations of Islam and the Orient, 1100–1450* (Cornell University Press, Ithaca, 2009), pp. 48–9.

19. Marco Polo, *The Travels*, trans. Ronald Latham (Penguin, London, 1958), p. 33.

20. Suzanne Conklin Akbari and Amilcare Iannucci (eds.), *Marco Polo and the Encounter of East and West* (University of Toronto Press, Toronto, 2008).

21. Quoted in Delno C. West, 'Christopher Columbus, Lost Biblical Sites and the Last Crusade', *The Catholic Historical Review*, 78, 4 (1992), pp. 519–41: p. 521.

22. Quoted in Scafi, *Mapping Paradise*, p. 242.

23. For the full text of the treaty see https://avalon.law.yale.edu/15th_century/mod001.asp.

24. Quoted in George Bruner Parks, *Richard Hakluyt and the English Voyages* (American Geographical Society, New York, 1928), p. 155.

25. Thomas Babington Macaulay, 'A Minute on Indian Education' (1835), quoted at: http://www.columbia.edu/itc/mealac/pritchett/00general links/macaulay/txt_minute_education_1835.html.

26. Walter Blanco and Jennifer T. Roberts (eds. and trans.), *The Histories: Herodotus* (Norton, New York, 2013), bk. 1, ch. 4, p. 6.

27. Quoted in Robert F. Brown and Peter C. Hodgson (eds.), *Hegel: Lectures on the Philosophy of World History*, vol. 1: *Manuscripts of the Introduction and the Lectures of 1822–1823* (Oxford University Press, Oxford, 2019), p. 211.

28. Quoted in A. L. Macfie (ed.), *Orientalism: A Reader* (Edinburgh University Press, Edinburgh, 2000), pp. 13–15.

29. Alison Stone, 'Hegel and Colonialism', *Hegel Bulletin*, 41, 2 (2020), pp. 247–70.

30. V. S. Naipaul, 'East Indian' (1965), in *Literary Occasions: Essays* (Vintage, London, 2003), pp. 38–41.

31. For the latest statistics see https://databank.worldbank.org/home.aspx.

32. Luke S. K. Wong, 'What's in a Name? Zhongguo (or "Middle Kingdom") Reconsidered', *The Historical Journal*, 58, 3 (2015), pp. 781–804.

SOUTH

1. Susan Sontag, *The Volcano Lover: A Romance* (Jonathan Cape, London, 1992), pp. 225–7.

2. Quoted in Antonio Gramsci, 'The Southern Question' (1926), https://cpb-us-e1.wpmucdn.com/blogs.uoregon.edu/dist/f/6855/files/2014/03/gramsci-southern-question1926-2jf8c5x.pdf, p. 4.

3. Salman Rushdie, 'In the South', *The New Yorker* (18 May 2009).

4. Maarten J. Raven, 'Egyptian Concepts of the Orientation of the Human Body', *The Journal of Egyptian Archaeology*, 91 (2005), pp. 37–53.

5. Yi-Fu Tuan, *Topophilia: A Study of Environmental Perception, Attitudes and Values* (Columbia University Press, New York, 1974), pp. 86–8.

6. What follows draws on the recent work on Islamic mapping and cross-cultural influence, especially Karen C. Pinto, *Medieval Islamic Maps: An Exploration* (University of Chicago Press, Chicago, 2006), Yossef Rapoport, *Islamic Maps* (Bodleian Library, Oxford, 2020), Nadja Danilenko, *Picturing the Islamicate World* (Koninklijke Brill, Leiden, 2021), and Marietta Stephaniants, 'The Encounter of Zoroastrianism with Islam', *Philosophy East and West*, 52 (2002), pp. 159–72.

7. Quoted in Danilenko, *Picturing the Islamicate World*, p. 65.

8. On the hemispherical map, its orientation and its transcriptions, see Dale Kedwards, *The Mappae Mundi of Medieval Iceland* (Boydell & Brewer, Cambridge, 2020), pp. 23–62, 115–18, 187–91.

9. Chen, 'Cardinal Meanings', p. 235.

10. James Legge (ed. and trans.), 'The Doctrine of the Mean', in *The Chinese Classics*, vol. 1: *The Four Books: Confucian Analects, The Great Learning,*

The Doctrine of the Mean, and the Works of Mencius (Clarendon Press, Oxford, 1892), pp. 389–90. I am grateful to Tim Brook for this reference.

11. Stephen A. Barney, W. J. Lewis, J. A. Beach and Oliver Berghof (eds. and trans.), *The Etymologies of Isidore of Seville* (Cambridge University Press, Cambridge, 2008), book XIII. 1. 6, p. 271.

12. Paul H. D. Kaplan, 'Magi, Winds, Continents: Dark Skin and Global Allegory in Early Modern Images', in Maryanne Cline Horowitz and Louise Arizzoli (eds.), *Bodies and Maps: Early Modern Personifications of the Continents* (Brill, Leiden, 2021), pp. 130–56.

13. Alexander Dalrymple, *An Account of the Discoveries Made in the South Pacifick Ocean, previous to 1764* (London, 1767), p. 89.

14. *Captain Cook's Journal During his first Voyage around the World made in H.M. Bark 'Endeavour', 1768–1771* (Elliot Stock, London, 1893), p. 228.

15. Quoted in Merlin Coverley, *South* (Oldcastle Books, London, 2016), p. 82.

16. Alexander von Humboldt, *Personal Narrative of Travels to the Equinoctal Regions of the New Continent during the years 1799–1804*, trans. Helen Maria Williams (Carrey, Philadelphia, 1815), pp. 240–41. I am grateful to Andrea Wulf for providing me with this and other references.

17. Robert Falcon Scott, *Journals: Captain Scott's Last Expedition* (Oxford University Press, Oxford, 2005), p. 113.

18. Elizabeth Leane, *Antarctica in Fiction: Imaginative Narratives of the Far South* (Cambridge University Press, Cambridge, 2012), pp. 55–6.

19. Quoted in Coverley, *South*, p. 164.

20. Quoted in Aarnoud Rommens, 'Latin American Abstraction: Upending Joaquín Torres-García's *Inverted Map*', *Mosaic: An Interdisciplinary Critical Journal*, 51, 2 (2028), pp. 35–58: p. 36.

21. The report was published as *North–South – A Program for Survival: The Report of the Independent Commission on International Development Issues under the Chairmanship of Willy Brandt* (MIT Press, Massachusetts, 1980). On the report and its limitations see Marcin Wojciech Solarz, 'North–South, Commemorating the First Brandt Report: Searching for the Contemporary Spatial Picture of the Global Rift', *Third World Quarterly*, 33, 3 (2012), pp. 559–69.

22. *North–South*, p. 7.

23. *North–South*, quoted at: https://sharing.org/information-centre/reports/brandt-report-summary.

24. https://www.lemonde.fr/en/international/article/2023/03/16/mia-mottley-leader-of-barbados-makes-global-south-s-concerns-heard-in-the-north_6019622_4.html; https://latinarepublic.com/2022/11/08/mia-mottley-prime-minister-of-barbados-speaks-at-the-opening-of-cop27/.

25. Jean and John Comaroff, *Theory from the South: Or, How Euro-America is Evolving Toward Africa* (Routledge, London, 2012), p. 7.

26. Mojisola Adebayo, 'Moj of the Antarctic: An African Odyssey', in *Mojisola Adebayo: Plays One* (Oberon, London, 2011), p. 58.

27. Adebayo, 'Moj of the Antarctic', p. 27.

28. Comaroff and Comaroff, *Theory from the South*, pp. 27, 47.

NORTH

1. Peter Davidson, *The Idea of North* (Reaktion Books, London, 2005).

2. Simon Armitage, *All Points North* (Penguin, London, 1998), pp. 16–17.

3. Michael Stausberg, 'Hell in Zoroastrian History', *Numen* 56, 2/3 (2009), pp. 217–53.

4. Quoted in Davidson, *The Idea of North*, p. 67.

5. B. L. Gordon, 'Sacred Directions, Orientation, and the Top of the Map', *History of Religions*, 10, 3 (1971), pp. 211–27: pp. 218–20.

6. Aristotle, *Meteorologica*, trans. H. D. P. Lee (Loeb, Harvard University Press, Cambridge, Massachusetts, 1952), bk. 2, ch. 1, p. 129.

7. Aristotle, *Meteorologica*, bk 2, ch. 6.

8. Blanco and Roberts (eds. and trans.), *Herodotus*, bk 4, ch. 36, p. 182.

9. Ian Whitaker, 'The Problem of Pytheas' Thule', *The Classical Journal*, 77, 2 (1981), pp. 148–64.

10. Gordon, 'Sacred Directions', pp. 220–21; Davidson, *The Idea of North*, p. 40.

11. See 'north, adv., adj., and n.', *OED Online* (Oxford University Press),

and Kenneth Shields, 'Some Comments on Early Germanic Cardinal Direction Words', *Historische Sprachforschung*, 121 (2008), pp. 219–25.

12. *Hamlet*, Act II scene ii.

13. Interview with Alfred Hitchcock in Peter Bogdanovich, *Who the Devil Made It* (Knopf, New York, 1997), pp. 471–557: p. 531.

14. Tom Cohen, *Hitchcock's Cryptonomies* (University of Minnesota Press, Minneapolis, 2005), p. 53. See also Stanley Cavell, 'North by Northwest', *Critical Inquiry*, 7, 4 (1981), pp. 761–76.

15. All subsequent quotes from the map's legends are taken from the anonymous article, 'Text and Translation of the Legends of the Original Chart of the World by Gerhard Mercator Issued in 1569', *Hydrographic Review*, 9 (1932), pp. 7–45.

16. Quoted in E. G. R. Taylor, 'A Letter Dated 1577 from Mercator to John Dee', *Imago Mundi*, 13 (1956), pp. 56–68: p. 57.

17. On the Selden Map see Robert Batchelor, 'The Selden Map Rediscovered: A Chinese Map of East Asian Shipping Routes, *c.* 1619', *Imago mundi*, 65, 1 (2013), pp. 37–63, and Timothy Brook, *Mr Selden's Map of China: The Spice Trade, a Lost Chart and the South China Sea* (Profile, London, 2014).

18. Quoted in Davidson, *The Idea of North*, p. 196.

19. Michael Jeremy and Michael Ernst Robinson, *Ceremony and Symbolism in the Japanese Home* (Manchester University Press, Manchester, 1989), p. 132.

20. Janice Cavell, 'The Sea of Ice and the Icy Sea: The Arctic Frame of *Frankenstein*', *Arctic*, 70, 3 (2017), pp. 295–307.

21. Philip Pullman, *The Golden Compass* (Knopf, New York, 1995), p. 78.

22. Michael Bravo and Sverker Sörlin, 'Narrative and Practice: An Introduction', in Bravo and Sörlin (eds.), *Narrating the Arctic: A Cultural History of Nordic Scientific Practices* (Watson, Massachusetts, 2002), p. 3, and Michael Bravo, *North Pole: Nature and Culture* (Reaktion, London, 2019), pp. 21–2. Much of what follows is indebted to Bravo's definitive work on the region. I am grateful to him for extensive communication and references on the subject.

23. Robert McGhee et al., 'Disease and the Development of Inuit Culture', *Current Anthropology*, 35, 5 (1994), pp. 565–94: p. 571.

24. MacDonald, *Arctic Sky*, pp. 169–70.

25. MacDonald, *Arctic Sky*, p. 173.

26. Quoted in M. R. O'Connor, *Wayfinding: The Science and Mystery of how Humans Navigate the World* (St Martin's, New York, 2019), p. 79.

27. Chauncey C. Loomis, 'The Arctic Sublime', in U. C. Knoepflmacher and G. B. Tennyson (eds.), *Nature and the Victorian Imagination* (University of California Press, Berkeley and Los Angeles, 1977), pp. 95–112.

28. John Kofron, 'Dickens, Collins, and the Influence of the Arctic', *Dickens Studies Annual*, 40 (2009), pp. 81–93.

29. Andrew Wawn, *Vikings and the Victorians* (Boydell and Brewer, Cambridge, 2000).

30. Geoffrey G. Field, 'Nordic Racism', *Journal of the History of Ideas*, 38, 3 (1977), pp. 523–40.

31. Quoted in Lisa Bloom, *Gender on Ice: American Ideologies of Polar Expeditions* (University of Minneapolis Press, Minneapolis, 1993), p. 47.

32. Commander R. E. Peary, 'The Lure of the North Pole', *Pall Mall* (1 October 1906), accessed at: https://archive.macleans.ca/article/1906/10/01/the-lure-of-the-north-pole.

33. Peary, 'Lure'.

34. Quoted in Bravo, *North Pole*, p. 186.

35. Peary, 'Lure'.

36. Frederick A. Cook, *My Attainment of the Pole* (Polar Publishing, New York, 1911), p. 27.

37. Quoted in Bloom, *Gender on Ice*, p. 48.

38. Matthew Henson, *A Negro Explorer at the North Pole* (Frederick Stokes, New York, 1912), p. 136.

39. Robert Stepto, *From Behind the Veil: A Study of Afro-American Narrative* (University of Illinois Press, Urbana, 1991), p. 67.

40. Quoted in Lisa E. Bloom, *Climate Change and the New Polar Aesthetics: Artists Reimagine the Arctic and Antarctic* (Duke University Press, London, 2002), p. 76.

41. Mojisola Adebayo, 'Matt Henson, North Star', in *Mojisola Adebayo: Plays One* (Oberon, London, 2011), pp. 258, 283.

42. Quoted in Davidson, *The Idea of North*, p. 108.

43. Quoted in Davidson, *The Idea of North*, p. 108.

44. W. H. Auden, *A Certain World: A Commonplace Book* (London, 1971), pp. 22–4.

45. Seamus Heaney, 'North' in *North* (Faber, London, 1975).

46. Louis-Edmond Hamelin, *Canadian Nordicity: It's Your North, Too* (Harvest House, Montreal, 1979).

47. Amanda Graham, 'Indexing the North: Broadening the Definition', *The Northern Review*, 6 (1990), pp. 21–37.

48. Glenn Gould, 'The Idea of the North', broadcast 28 December 1967, Canadian Broadcasting Corporation. All subsequent quotes are taken from the transcript accessed at: https://sites.google.com/site/ggfminor/home/idea-of-north-transcript.

49. Margaret Atwood, *Strange Things: The Malevolent North in Canadian Literature* (Clarendon Press, Oxford, 1995), p. 140. I am grateful to Tim Brook for this reference.

50. Atwood, *Strange Things*, p. 22.

51. Atwood, *Strange Things*, p. 101.

52. Robert A. Brightman, 'The Windigo in the Material World', *Ethnohistory*, 35, 4 (1988), pp. 337–79.

53. Jack D. Forbes, *Columbus and the Cannibals: The Wétiko Disease of Exploitation, Imperialism and Terrorism*, rev. edn (Seven Stories, New York, 2008).

54. Atwood, *Strange Things*, p. 124.

55. Atwood, *Strange Things*, p. 140.

56. Atwood, *Strange Things*, p. 140.

57. Peter Wadhams, *A Farewell to Ice: A Report from the Arctic* (Penguin, London, 2017), p. 84.

58. Wadhams, *Farewell to Ice*, p. 202.

WEST

1. Yoshitake, 'Japanese Names for the Four Cardinal Points', pp. 100–102.

2. John Roberts, *The Triumph of the West* (BBC Books, London, 1985), p. 431.

3. Robert H. Fuson, 'The Orientation of Mayan Ceremonial Centers', *Annals of the Association of American Geographers*, 59, no. 3 (1969), pp. 494–511, 502.

4. Mietzner and Pasch, 'Expressions of Cardinal Directions', p. 5.

5. Loren Baritz, 'The Idea of the West', *The American Historical Review*, 66, 3 (1961), pp. 618–40: pp. 620–21.

6. Homer, *The Odyssey*, trans. Robert Fagles (Viking, New York, 1996), bk 4, lines 636–9.

7. Hesiod, 'Works and Days' in M. L. West (ed. and trans.), Hesiod, *Theogony and Works and Days* (Oxford University Press, Oxford, 1988), ll. 168–72.

8. Hesiod, 'Theogony', in M. L. West (ed. and trans.), Hesiod, *Theogony and Works and Days* (Oxford University Press, Oxford, 1988), ll. 215–16.

9. Tom Moylan, 'Irish Voyages and Visions: Pre-figuring, Re-configuring Utopia', *Utopian Studies*, 18, 3 (2007), pp. 299–323.

10. Quoted in Moylan, 'Irish Voyages', p. 299.

11. Quoted in Baritz, 'Idea of the West', p. 621.

12. Seneca, *Seneca's Tragedies*, trans. Frank Justus Miller (Heinemann, London, 1960), vol. 1, pp. 260–61.

13. *The Etymologies of Isidore of Seville*, 'The Cosmos and its Parts', ed. and trans. Stephen Barney et al. (Cambridge University Press, Cambridge, 2002), bk. XIII, 1, p. 271.

14. Quoted in Brotton, *Twelve Maps*, p. 105.

15. Quoted in Baritz, 'Idea of the West', p. 631.

16. Quoted in Baritz, 'Idea of the West', p. 632.

17. Timothy Brook, *Great State: China and the State* (Profile, London, 2019), pp. 207–12.

18. Brook, *Great State*, pp. 226–7.

19. Richard Hakluyt, *A Discourse of Western Planting* (London, 1584).

20. Samuel Purchas, *Purchas His Pilgrimes* (London, 1625), in *Hakluytus Posthumus*, 20 vols. (James MacLehose, Glasgow, 1905–7), vol. 1, p. 173.

21. Quoted in Baritz, 'Idea of the West', p. 636.

22. George Herbert, 'The Church Militant' in *The Temple: Sacred Poems and Private Ejaculations* (Cambridge, 1633), p. 184.

23. Quoted in Baritz, 'Idea of the West', p. 637.

24. Rexmond C. Cochrane, 'Bishop Berkeley and the Progress of Arts and Learning: Notes on a Literary Convention', *Huntingdon Library Quarterly*, 17, 3 (1954), pp. 229–49.

25. https://www.ushistory.org/declaration/related/proc63.html.

26. Roger Cushing Aikin, 'Paintings of Manifest Destiny: Mapping the Nation', *American Art*, 14, 3 (2000), pp. 78–89.

27. Quoted in Jochen Wierich, 'Struggling through History: Emanuel Leutze, Hegel, and Empire', *American Art*, 15, 2 (2001), pp. 52–71: p. 66, and G. A. Kelly, 'Hegel's America', *Philosophy & Public Affairs*, 2, 1 (1972), pp. 3–36.

28. Wierich, 'Struggling through History', p. 66.

29. Kelly, 'Hegel's America', p. 3.

30. Robert C. Williams, *Horace Greeley: Champion of American Freedom* (New York University Press, New York, 2006), pp. 40–41.

31. Frederick J. Turner, 'The Significance of the Frontier in American History' (1893): https://www.historians.org/about-aha-and-membership/aha-history-and-archives/historical-archives/the-significance-of-the-frontier-in-american-history-(1893).

32. Henry David Thoreau, 'Walking', *The Atlantic Monthly*, 9, 56 (June 1862), pp. 657–74: p. 657.

33. Thoreau, 'Walking', p. 665.

34. Andrew Menard, 'Nationalism and the Nature of Thoreau's "Walking"', *The New England Quarterly*, 85, 4 (2012), pp. 591–621.

35. Thoreau, 'Walking', p. 662.

36. Thoreau, 'Walking', p. 663.

37. Thoreau, 'Walking', p. 663.

38. Thoreau, 'Walking', p. 662.

39. See 'west, adv., adj., n.1, and prep', *OED Online* (Oxford University Press).

40. Quoted in Alastair Bonnett, *The Idea of the West: Culture, Politics and History* (Palgrave, Basingstoke, 2004), p. 67.

41. Quoted in Bonnett, *Idea of the West*, p. 69.

42. Oswald Spengler, *The Decline of the West*, 2 vols. (first published 1923, Alfred Knopf, New York, 1928), vol. 1, p. 3.

43. Spengler, *Decline*, vol. 1, p. 31.

44. Spengler, *Decline*, vol. 1, p. 5; vol. 2, p. 506.

45. Robert Merry, 'Spengler's Ominous Prophecy', *The National Interest*, 123 (2 January 2013), pp. 11–22.

46. Bill Ashcroft, Gareth Griffiths and Helen Tiffin, *The Empire Writes Back: Theory and Practice in Post-Colonial Literatures* (Routledge, London, 1989).

47. Ian Buruma and Avishai Margalit, *Occidentalism: The West in the Eyes of its Enemies* (Penguin, London, 2004).

48. Seyyed Jalāl Āl-e Ahmad, *Occidentosis: A Plague from the West*, trans. R. Campbell (Mizan Press, Berkeley, California, 1984), p. 28.

49. Richard Rodriguez, 'True West: Relocating the Horizon of the American Frontier', *Harper's Magazine* (1 September 1996), pp. 17–46: pp. 17, 44, 45. I am grateful to Rob Nixon for this reference.

50. Rodriguez, 'True West', pp. 44, 46.

THE BLUE DOT

1. Bond, *Wayfinding*, and O'Connor, *Wayfinding*.

2. Eleanor A. Maguire, Katherine Woollett and Hugo J. Spiers, 'London Taxi Drivers and Bus Drivers: A Structural MRI and Neuropsychological Analysis', *Hippocampus*, 16, 12 (2006), pp. 1091–1101.

3. Bond, *Wayfinding*, pp. 217–18.

Index